JESUS AND ME

Volume One

Maria Iskander

Copyright

JESUS AND ME (JAM) BOOK
VOLUME ONE

First published 2023

ISBN: 978-0-6457342-8-7

Disclaimer: Dear readers, this book is only a starting point for your deep reading and comprehension of the Holy Bible. In other words, this book IS NOT a replacement of the God inspired scriptures. Please know that the Holy Bible scriptures are a reliable source of truth and wisdom because it came directly from God Himself. Perfect. Nevertheless, may you read the JAM book for inspiration to commit in reading the Holy Bible -daily- with everlasting joy and peace.

Published with the assistance of Angel Key Publications
https://angelkey.com.au

Angel Key
Publications

Contents

Acknowledgement

I acknowledge and value the cultural histories, heritage, and traditions of Aboriginal and Torres Strait Islander people. It is my hope that you will join my vision to educate ourselves, our families, and our greater community about unity, understanding, acceptance and meaningful connections.

Dedication

I dedicate this book to my brother- stunning, kind and courageous- John Iskander.

The Pentateuch

Adam and Eve

In the Garden of Eden there once lived a man.
This man named Adam, created from clay by God's hands.
Surrounded by beautiful nature and animals too.
Adam was happy but felt a little taboo.
There was not one animal that he looked alike.
So Adam began to feel something was not right.
Then God sent Adam to go down and sleep.
And as Adam slept, God made the woman Eve.
The next morning Adam woke up to find.
A beautiful woman, the first of humankind.

The first man and woman lived in harmony.
Causing a cunning snake to be in envy.
Then one day as Eve was collecting fruit.
The evil snake crept and spoke not the truth.
Eve was deceived and disobeyed God's rule.
She ate of the Forbidden tree and then Adam too.

God was upset that their pleasure overcame them.
Leading to their exile from the Garden of Eden.

Yet, after their exile God choose to forgive.
Giving Adam and Eve a second chance to live.

It would be a matter of time when God would provide.
A hero – our Lord Jesus Christ, the saviour of mankind.

The Story of Cain And Abel

Soon after Adam and Eve sinned.
They gave birth to two sons in their kin.
The firstborn Cain was a farmer.
Leaving Abel a shepherd, as he'd prefer.

Both sons brought a sacrifice to the Lord.
But God accepted Abel's much more.
Abel brought the firstborn of his flock.
But Cain, brought some harvest-not a lot.
Abel's heart was in his sacrifice to the Lord.
Whereas Cain did his sacrifice, as if bored.

God's favour to Abel for being zealous.
Lead Cain to become dangerously jealous.
So as Abel was shepherding, Cain killed him.
And immediately Cain wanted to hide his sin.

As God saw Cain's sin, He knew he took Abel's life.
God placed a red cross on Cain, for the rest of his life.

Again God had mercy on Adam and Eve.
Giving them another son to aid their grief.
The son named Seth was appointed to replace.
And expected to crush the serpent's head someday.

Noah's Ark and The Flood

God being merciful and good,
Gave timeless chances so people would,

Repent and turn back from their sins.
Sadly, no one was good, besides Noah's kin.

So God assigned Noah and his family to build.
A huge ark that would take over 100 years to yield.
The evil people laughed all those years on Noah's ark.
Until the joke was on them, as the rain poured hard.

The animals came two by two inside.
Before it began to rain for non-stop.
Noah, his family and the animals in the ark alone.
Leaving the foolish people drowning in their homes.

For forty days and nights the rain lasted.
Until finally a dove God-sent , had presented.
The dove gave Noah an olive leaf , a sign of land and flew.
And when the dove didn't return, Noah knew.

Land finally at sight, Noah could finally disembark.
Along with his family and the animals in the ark.
A fresh start for renewed mankind came at last.
And God promised by a rainbow, that He would,
Never flood the entire world again for good

Father Abraham Had Many Sons

A long time ago, there once lived a man.
His name Abram, before changed to Father Abraham.
God and he would talk face to face.
And Abram obeyed God with haste.
He obeyed God when He told him to move.
Leaving all behind, with his wife Sarai and some food.

Abram believed in God's promises too.
Including the birth of a son to come through.
One day, God appeared in the form of three men.

Declaring Sarai would give birth and when.
Isaac was born when Sarai was 100 years old.
Truly age and time could not stop God at all.
God's covenant was fulfilled and names changed.
Abram to Father Abraham and Sarai to Sarah the same.

God Testing Father Abraham

Father Abraham waited so many years for a son.
When Isaac finally came, he rejoiced with everyone.
Then God wanted to put Father Abraham's love to the test.
So God asked Father Abraham to sacrifice Isaac with no relent.

At first Father Abraham felt confused but He continued to trust.
After all if God requires this sacrifice, to follow it – one must.
Without further ado, Father Abraham took Isaac and they walked.
When they reached the mountain tops, Father Abraham then talked.
Father Abraham told Isaac that he would be the sacrifice as God willed.
And Isaac obeyed with no hesitation at the knowledge he'd be killed.

Right before Father Abraham made the first blow on Isaac's chest.
An angel of God revealed to him that he had passed God's test.
God's test was to see if Father Abraham loved him with all his heart.
So as Isaac was saved, Father Abraham sacrificed a ram found from the start.

Sodom and Gomorrah

The cities of Sodom and Gomorrah,
May have had walls and buildings taller,
Yet they decided to choose evil,
So God saved only Father Abraham's people.
From Father Abraham's kin, to his nephew Lot,
All were saved, before the cities became naught.

At the land of Sodom and Gomorrah two angels trod.
And went to spend the night at the house of Lot.
Lot knew the evil in Sodom and Gomorrah as well.

In return for Lot's faithfulness, the angels went to tell.
Lot and his family from the evil city to flee with haste.
As God would destroy the city and everyone in place.

To begin with Lot was afraid and crippled with shock.
Until the angels persuaded him to leave his life stock.
As Lot and his family journeyed out to safe land.
Not one looked back, following the angles command.

Yet, Lot's wife filled with no self-control to halt.
Dared to look back- so she turned to a pillar of salt.

Isaac and Rebekah

Isaac met Rebekah at the well,
A love at first sight, all was swell.
Uncle Laban encouraged the wedlock,
Of Isaac and Rebekah in front of God.

After many joyous years passed,
Isaac and Rebekah had children at last.
Two sons , both wonderful and sacred.
The oldest named Esau, the younger Jacob.

When Isaac was old and blind,
Esau lost his rightful birthright.
Alas, this happened through sham,
By Rebekah and Jacob's hand.

Jacob and Rachel

Jacob left with the birthright,
And journeyed to find a wife.
While working for his uncle Lavan
He asked for Rachel's hand.

Lavan accepted with one condition,
To work for seven years all in.
After that, Jacob was misled,
To marrying Leah instead.

So Jacob worked another seven years,
To marry Rachel finally, for real.
Marriage bells rung to Jacob's delight,
As Jacob wed Rachel- the love of his life.

Joseph's Journey

Jacob had twelve sons in time,
Ten were from Leah's line.
Leaving only two from Rachel,
Joseph was the son treated as special.

Jacob gave Joseph a lovely coat,
Of many colours and tones.
This made Joseph's brothers jealous
So they sold him with callous.

The brothers then lied to Jacob,
That Joseph didn't make it.
Jacob and Rachel wept bitterly,
Their hearts were broken entirely.

Joseph being sold in Egypt as a slave,
Remained courageous and brave.
God gifted Joseph with reading dreams,
A gift that made him successful with ease.

From reading dreams on things to come in,
He prepared Egypt for a long famine.
The pharaoh was so impressed by his charm.
So he made Joseph his second man in charge.
Joseph now being a great leader,
Tricked his brothers- who were weaker.
When his brothers finally realised,
They embraced Joseph and cried.

Up till now Joseph forgave them,
And gave them food for the famine.
Jacob rejoiced knowing Joseph was well,
Then blessed his sons and said his farewell.

Joseph and his brothers mourned for days,
As they buried Jacob, their father, in the grave.
Joseph stressed to his brothers to not be afraid
And that their sins against him, he forgave.

Beautiful Child

In Egypt during a dark time,
When Israelite babies would die
A beautiful child was able to survive,
Thanks to an Egyptian princess so kind.

The Pharaonic family named him Moses,
They brought him up in love and closeness.
Until Moses grew up of age
He left Pharaoh's palace and ran away.
Moses kept running 'til he lost his breath,
Meeting Jethro who he loved to death.
Jethro gave Moses his daughter to marry,
And they lived together so happy.

The Burning Bush

One day when Moses was tending the sheep
God appeared in a burning bush, fiery in heat.
Moses was instructed to free the Israelites,
From their bitter slavery in Egypt all this time.

A total of ten plagues occurred so vast
The Pharaoh was stubborn to pass,
Only until the final plague was done,
Were the Israelites' freedom finally won.

As the Israelites were speedily departing,
Moses' staff and God made the Red Sea parted.
The Israelites crossed the Red Sea safe and sound,
Free from the perils of Pharaoh and his crowd.

Much later at Mount Sinai,
Moses received God's law inscribed.
However, the Israelites fell in shame
By worshiping idols once again.
So Moses broke the tablets in rage.
Leaving God to give him another two,
With hopes that it would be followed through.

Leviticus Express

The holiness of God is evident,
Calling for the Israelites to repent.
Sacrifices became the foundational utility
To be practised by the Levite priests only.

Following God's sacrificial guidelines,
The offerings were done on time.
Atonement of sins was received at once,
Through the shedding of the animal's blood.
This sacrificial blood reconciled,

God with His people in hindsight.
The Israelites were finally pure again,
Cleansed by this atonement of their sin.
Also, the priests and Israelites would tithe generously
Leading God to reward them tremendously.

Four

Numbers being the fourth book,
Shows the journey the Israelites took
A total of forty years they wandered in the wilderness,
Until reaching the Canaan- as God promised.

Funny that it could have taken only 11 days,
But did not because the Israelites rebelled and complained.

The book is also called Numbers for the purpose,
Of God ordering the people under a consensus.
A total of twelve tribes were distinguished in Israel,
God filled these tribes with strength and power as well.

Love and Obey God

To rebel or obey God, the choice is ours.
The Israelites chose to at first be cowards,
To be ignorant and foolish to rebel God's power,
Leaving them to travel very long and tiring hours.

Total of 40 years did the Israelites journey,
All because they didn't obey the law fully.
God gave them the law and they chose to disobey,
It broke God to see them choosing corruption as a way.

In spite of God's warnings time over time,
The Israelites still worshipped idols with pride.
Not even Moses survived to see the Promised land,
God took his soul at 120 years, making Joshua son of Nun in command.

The second generation of Israelites were successful to see,
This Promised land planned by God for them, from eternity.

Moses' song was sung in remembrance of the other Israelites,
Serving as a reminder to love and obey God with your life.

Joshua and God's Gift To Israel

Canaan was given as a gift to Israel,
To save them from loss and exile.
However, to prosper in the land,
The Israelites had to obey God's command.

The Israelites at times also rebelled,
So God had to teach them as well.
Through conquest and exiles
The Israelites learnt to do right.

With Joshua's speeches and warnings,
The Israelites then went in mourning.
So that the gift of the land wouldn't be threatened
God took heed to the Israelites' cry
And their sincere repentance time after time.

Joshua was truly a good leader and man,
By following God's expectations in Canaan.
The divine retributions from God still gave space,
For God's final word and unconditional grace.

Judges - Deliverance and Mercy

The consistent pattern followed in all chapters,
Involves people's unfaithfulness and repentance after.
When unfaithful to God, the people were shamed.
But when back to God, the people were saved.

All the judges assigned by God, helped to deliver,

The Israelites from oppression and enemies so sinister.

From Othniel, Chushan , Ehud, Eglon and Aram
To Samson, Gideon, Abimelech and Jephthah.
All other minor judges were also prosperous in peace,
From the North to the South of Israel, to the West and East.

A woman as well was a champion judge that delivered,
Going by the name of Deborah, no judge could be bettered.
Only the minor judges could do actual legal judgements,
Yet, Deborah being a major judge, didn't stop for making justice.

Where You Go I Will Go

There once lived a Moabite named Ruth,
She was beautiful and married too.
Alas, when her husband Mahlon died,
Ruth and Naomi- her mother- in- law cried.

After the days of mourning were spent,
Ruth promised to stay where Naomi went.
So after farewelling Orpah, they left,
On a journey from Moab to Bethlehem.

Boaz was an owner of a field there,
And he was kind to Ruth and cared.
Boaz made sure Ruth had extra grain
As she was gleaned the crops away.

Sooner or later, Boaz and Ruth married,
The marriage made Naomi very happy.
They bore a son and named him Obed,
The future ancestor of the son of God.

I Won't Be Childless
(Ref: 1 Samuel, Chapter 1)

Day by day,
And year by year,
Hannah patiently prayed.
Shedding many tears.
After Hannah's long barrenness,
She bore a son- as God promised.

Hannah called her only son -Samuel.
A name meaning "God Heard".
For God heard her,
According to His will.

Soon after Samuel's miraculous birth,
Hannah gave him away to Eli the priest.
With Eli, Samuel served Yahweh,
With diligence and mirth.
Samuel's service never ceased.

From praying, fasting, and praising,
Samuel learnt how to be wise.

Yet remained humble,
In all the days of his life.

Honour You ((Ref: 1 Samuel, Chapter 2)

Hannah gives God thanks,
By reciting a hymn.
Alas, Eli's sons deviate,
Displaying corruption.

After Eli's sons stole meat
And in the temple, sleep,
An angel appeared to Eli, with a warning.
Eli's sons were punished according.

Eli's Fate (Ref: 1 Samuel, Chapter 3)

Yahweh appeared to Samuel, foretelling Eli's fate.
Although Samuel was anxious about it,
He told Eli the bad news, straight away.
Alas, Eli's sons did not change or come clean.
So, Eli lost his two sons for eternity.
This heartbreaking tragedy,
Fulfilled Yahweh's prophecies.

Israelites Defeated (Ref: 1 Samuel, Chapter 4)

In war with the Philistines,
The Israelites were despised.
After blood, sweat and a hard beat,
The Israelites faced terrible defeat.
So, the Israelites decided to change,
And take their Ark and pray.
Without a doubt, the Ark blessed.
Making the Israelites at rest.
But sadly, the Israelites routed,
And the Ark, by Philistines, was looted.

When Eli and his daughter-in-law heard this,
They both collapsed, dying from total sadness.

Ark of The Convenant (Ref: 1 Samuel, Chapter 5)

The treacherous Philistines,
Kept the Israelites' Ark in place,
Until they became very sick,
And later cried in fear,
"Oh, Israelites take the Ark back".
And they did with cheer.

Ark of The Lord (Ref: 1 Samuel, Chapter 6)

As the Philistines returned the ark.
The Beth Shemesh people had one wish:
That the poor dwellers of Kiriath Jearim,
Would remove the ark, from their midst.

Samuel For Help (Ref: 1 Samuel, Chapter 7)

Samuel exhorts the Israelites,
To abandon their idols, or face demise.
The Israelites listen and Yahweh is glad.
Such gladness ensured military success,
Against the Philistines, on Israel land.

Unhappy (Ref: 1 Samuel, Chapter 8)

God judges Samuel's sons: Joal and Abijah,
Miserably for Samuel, God rules them as corrupt,
This ruling left Samuel, feeling down and abrupt.

Spiritual Eyes (Ref: 1 Samuel, Chapter 9)

Saul searched for his father's lost donkeys.
Whilst looking, Saul happened to meet Samuel.

Samuel told him a set of prophecies.
Suggesting that Saul would be Israel's king.

Saul, Annointed King (Ref: 1 Samuel, Chapter 10)

Samuel anointed Saul as king.
Many events subsequently took place,
Yet Saul continued ruling everything.
And Mizbah announced Saul's kingship as: 'a rightful place'.

Saul's Victory (Ref: 1 Samuel, Chapter 11)

The Ammonites send many threats.
To torture the Jabesh Giled people
Saul gathers 330,000 troops -all the best.
Hence, defeating Saul's enemies with ease.

The Lord's Wait (Ref: 1 Samuel, Chapter 12)

Despite old age, Samuel delivers a harsh speech.
Criticising the people for requesting a king.
The people do not bother to repent or comprehend.
So, Samuel prays for a rainstorm, to scare them.

Battles (Ref: 1 Samuel, Chapter 13)

In response to Saul's offensive act,
The Philistines prepare to attack.
Saul assembles an army and offers a sacrifice.
But Samuel tells Saul to open his eyes.
Saul hears Samuel's fresh prophecy.
This time, about Saul's loss of monarchy.

A Foolish Oath (Ref: 1 Samuel, Chapter 14)

Sau's son –Jonathan, decided to leave the camp,
Killing twenty Philistine soldiers, by chance.
After this, the Philistines were in a panic.

Saul forbade eating for all members of his army.
And almost kills his own son, for eating honey.

The Noise Of Sheep And Animals (Ref: 1 Samuel, Chapter 15)

The Lord called Samuel,
For a great plan,
To make King Saul
Not fall,
But stand.
So, Samuel stood,
With no fear
And told King Saul
To attack,
The kingdom of
King Ama-lak.

So, King Saul went.
With brave men,
Ruddy soldiers,
Who attacked.
Destroying all.
Ama-lak children,
Women and men.

Alas, Saint Paul faulted,
In something small,
He smuggled goods,
And a choice animal.

God became angry,
So incredibly angry
With King Saul.
Then Samuel went
To announce

God's anger,
On King Saul,
And his accounts.

King Saul wept,
He could not believe,
That God would be,
Terribly displeased.

And Samuel mourned,
Every night and day,
For King Saul's fate.
Was about to change.

God Chooses David (Ref: 1 Samuel, Chapter 16)

Another day,
Another task,
For Samuel
To follow through.

Samuel took off,
At break of dawn,
Travelling afar,
He finally arrived.
To the house of Jesse,
Who welcomed him,
Taking Samuel inside.

"Peace be to your house"
Samuel warmly announced.
As Jesse called out his sons,
To be quickly pronounced.

God said no to Eliab,
Abindab

And Shammah too.
So, Samuel began to wonder,
Which of Jesse's seven sons,
Was God referring to?

Son after son was pronounced,
As utterly rejected.
Leaving Jesse feeling done,
And disrespected.

So, Samuel quietly prayed,
And God revealed to him:
That the youngest son of Jesse- David,
Was outside- shepherding.

At this revelation,
Samuel went to see,
This former shepherd boy-David
And anoint him now as King.

David And Goliath (Ref: 1 Samuel, Chapter 17)

Calmness in Israel,
Lasted for a time,
The Israelites were strong,
Good and full of life.

Oh, how wonderful it would be,
For this to last for eternity.
Yet, Israel was soon baffled.
By the Philistines- who called for
A strong and mighty battle.

The Philistines had a giant.
It was ugly and named Goliath.

This left the Israelites fearful,
Hopeless- expecting to die.

Against all the odds,
And with full accord.
David travelled fast,
He knew he had to do something,
He had to attack from afar.

So, with not a sword in sight,
Or armour to save him.
David took stones,
A slingshot,
And God, with him.

By the power of God,
David's slingshot flew.
Knocking down this Giant
Without further ado,

The Philistines wept,
They could not believe,
How their giant- Goliath,
Died of a slingshot, and so quickly.

The world was shocked for a moment,
On what David had done.
Leaving Israel in an uproar,
For they had finally won.

Love And War (Ref: 1 Samuel, Chapter 18)

Much of David's success
Was due to his charm.
People simply liked him.
For he was strong, yet calm.

Although Saul was handsome and tall.
David's fame in Israel grew more and more,
This made Saul very jealous.
For he could not understand
How and why people liked David,
After all, he was just a young man.

As a result, Saul made his son- Jonathan,
To reach a dead-end
Between Him- his father
Or David his friend

In a difficult place,
Jonathan finally chose,
To stay friends with David.
Forgetting his father's woes.

David Flees From Saul (Ref: 1 Samuel, Chapter 19)

Jonathan defends David,
Before soldiers and his father- Saul.
Jonathan made sure David,
Was protected from all.

Michal also helps David to flee,
From Israel to Ramah- a land far away.
As David fled and escaped safely.
Samuel gave David some certainty.

Samuel told David of God's plan.
And how God would protect him,
From Saul, a now wicked man.

Killer Instinct (Ref: 1 Samuel, Chapter 20)

The Spirit of God protected David,
In a powerful way.

David wanted to know if Saul,
And his hard heart, had changed.

Alas, Saul did not reconcile.
But rather kept scheming:
To make David disappear.
And take away his pride.

David checked in with Jonathan.
In order to make sure.
For he knew Jonathan, unlike his father Saul,
Was honourable and pure.

Jonathan continued to reassure David.
Offering David with great help
In skipping the New Moon Feast,
To protect himself.

David At Nob And Gath (Ref: 1 Samuel, Chapter 21)

In his hard situation, David visits a priest.
The priest named Ahimelech, hears David's plea.
From David explaining his issue with Saul.
It was clear that Saul's jealousy took a toll.

Adullam Cave (Ref: 1 Samuel, Chapter 22)

After dwelling with Ahimelech for a time,
David knew he had to find,
A new place, unknown, and for refuge.
So, he found a cave, where no one knew.
The cave was large and called Adullam.
It kept David safe, and free from harm.

David's family and friends later found the cave.
As they entered inside, they shared David's pain.

Later weeping, they decided to help David succeed,
Announcing him as their captain, for eternity.

David knew he was called by God to be king.
But he did not know what God would do.
For Saul killed all priests- but one,
That helped him flee,
Such horror and bloodshed,
Made David feel guilty.

Later, David prayed to God,
To keep his family protected,
And to keep them from harm.

Victory (Ref: 1 Samuel, Chapter 23)

God directs David to lead,
His mighty men and soldiers,
To defeat their enemies.

Following the battle against the Philistines,
And its victorious outcome,
David rescued the city of Keliah,
Saving the livelihood, of everyone.

In the Judean wilderness, David kept having narrow escapes,
From Saul's erotic, uncomfortable,
And almost, never-ending, chase.

If that was not enough to endure,
Brace yourselves, for there is more.
For David was also betrayed,
By the Ziphites,
Who were once his 'friends',
Oh, what a shame!

As Jonathan and David say their goodbyes,
Jonathan is apologies for his father's pride.
David pledges no harm but flees.

By God's light and grace,
David finally arrives,
At "The Rock of Escape",
With no harm in sight.

Glory To God (Ref: 1 Samuel, Chapter 24)

Now it happened, when Saul had returned,
That the Philistines raised with him, a familiar concern.
The Philistines announced David's dwelling in En Gedi.
In price for a crossfire, and a peace treaty.

Saul then took three thousand chosen men.
And the chase to kill David, started all over again.

Saul unknowingly comes to the same cave.
Where David and his men, were hiding away.
To be an example, to forgive all,
David restrains himself from killing Saul.

David only had cut a corner of Saul's robe,
To prove his godliness,
Zeal and focus, to pleasing God alone.

Afterwards, David went out of the cave,
And when Saul looked behind him,
David could tell that Saul was afraid.
"My Lord, I am your servant.
And I will do you no harm.
Although you plot to always kill me.
I know, you were chosen by God".

Truly, David showed great kindness to Saul.
For he knew very well that Saul was unwell.
Indeed, Saul was a lost cause due to actions,
And not from anyone else.

Apolegetic Abigial (Ref: 1 Samuel, Chapter 25)

David asks Nabal for provisions,
Of food, water, and other supplies
For Israel's Kingdom.
In full rage, Nabal rejected to assist.
Leaving David enraged,
And unwilling to forgive.

At this event, Abigail came,
To deliver her husband-Nabal, from blame.
In purity of heart and full faith,
Abigail stood before David, and proclaimed:

"Oh my King, please forgive my husband's debt.
His unkind words, I do regret.
But please now accept these supplies, as a gift.
For I will give you honour, as long as I live".

This great act of kindness,
And extra mile. '
Made David forgive Nabal,
And even smile.

By the hand of God alone,
Nabal died, the next day.

As wise Abigail was finally free
David got to marry her happily.

David's Spare (Ref: 1 Samuel, Chapter 26)

Saul chases after David.
Some things never change.
David sneaks into the Saul's chambers,
To steal Saul's personal items away.

In secret, David returns to his camp.
Gifting his soldiers with the items,
He stole from Saul's hand.

Although David did this crime,
Saul feels content this time.

As Saul learned that David again,
Had the opportunity to kill
But again, chose not to,
Following through God's will.

Relentless Pursuit Ref: 1 Samuel, Chapter 27)

Fleeing from Israel to Philistia,
David plunders away.
Combined with Judah and neighbouring cities around,
David manages to raid.

Murky Mediums Ref: 1 Samuel, Chapter 28)

The Philistines prepare to attack,
The tribe of Israel, and its' army.

So, with merciless combat.
Saul vows to ensure victory
For Israel and its' army.

Saul then travels to En Dor
Where a ghost is conjured.

The ghost was revealed as Samuel,
A prophet, righteous and pure.

Soon after, Samuel reveals to Saul, his fate.
Confirming his doom- a defeated state.
Though Saul is distraught by the news.
Saul stubbornly decides to fight,
For he had nothing to lose.

God Protected (Ref: 1 Samuel, Chapter 29)

With David in their ranks privately,
The Philistines start to prepare,
For an unrequited victory.

As a result, David's loyalty to Israel, is disbelieved.
Leaving him with only one option to keep alive.
That option was to leave Israel immediately,
And so, David did just that,
In full wisdom, hope and dignity.

Strenghtened In The Lord (Ref: 1 Samuel, Chapter 30)

David and his men return to Ziklag
Finding their homes burned bad.

If that was not enough
David and his men also discovered,
That their possessions were stolen,
And their families were kidnapped,
Scattered all from another.

David and his men pursue the culprit of the crime.
Announcing and plotting revenge.
Merciless and swift revenge,
To the people of Amalekite.

The Philistines' Fight With Israel (Ref: 1 Samuel, Chapter 31)

Battle scars to and fro.
Soldiers annihilating in every blow.
With no hope left to succeed,
Saul realises that he will in fact die- eventually.

Indeed, when Saul witnesses' death after death,
Inclusive of his son- Jonathan.
Saul then requests to be slayed.
By the hand of a soldier.
Who was near his way.

The Philistines were glad as they won.
For the war was tough on everyone.

Saul and his son-Jonathan, have their bodies vandalized,
By the wicked and merciless Philistines.
When David finds out of this horrid event,
King David buries the bodies in Gilead,
With full love, honour,
And no ounce of contempt.

Joel Detailing The Day of The Lord

Joel's prophetic judgements date from 835BC,
With focus on worship in the Jerusalem city.
Identified as the beloved son of Pethuel,
Joel commented and preached a great deal.

Joel, being one of the earliest prophets,
Frequently referenced Zion with context.
This canon of scripture, mentions a biblical idea,
Being the day of the Lord coming near.

Joel suggests on how to prepare on the way,
Striking rituals of all kinds relevant to us today.
By referring to the locust plague, Joel was able,
To imprint the Lord's judgement to the faithful.

Like a brand of sears from animal flesh.
The Lord's judgement moved all to repent.
Such repentance lead to a period of purification,
And the restoration for people of all nations.

Obadiah's Lowly Message

Obadiah's name meaning Yahweh's messenger
Offers a lowly message for people to remember.
As a faithful prophet, Obadiah humbly preached,
God's judgement on Edom and Judah southeast.

Edom was found guilty of pride before God,
Exemplifying that pride taints a pure heart.
Through Obadiah, the Edomites were reminded,
To stop mistreating all of humankind.

Obadiah's message was significant for the Edomites,
Renewing their relationship with God in their life.
Truly Obadiah's lowly message had an impact,
Brining all nations, primarily Judah and Edom,
Finding themselves with God, restored and strong.

Nahum- A Light in The Darkness

Nahum wrote on God's goodness and strength,
After two hundred years under Assyrian reign.
This was a time of darkness and cultural compromise.
As the Ninevites lost their spiritual eyes.

Nahum's prophecy against the city of Ninevites ,
Inspired repentance from idolatry of all kinds.
Besides Nahum showing God's concern over sin,
He comforted them with God's desire to forgive.

Nahum preached that God is always right,
And that He will always show mercy every time.
This book also details God as dealing others as equal,
Passing comfort in all situations, for His people.

Habakkuk's Capital Reminder

Habakkuk was a professional prophet,
Trained in the law from Moses' ministry.
He wrote at a time of Judah's ruin,
Describing Judah's low time in history.

In the first five years of Jehoiakim's reign (609–598 BC),
Habakkuk's prophecies directed,
God's people to be faithful again.
Saved from sin, redeemed and protected.

Habakkuk's prophecy and prayer witnesses,
God's undying love and steadfast promises.
It paints a picture that God may look silent,
But in fact, always has plans to deal with tyrants.

Habakkuk's example encourages us all to believe,
That God's will, is always be good for us to proceed.
Even when we see and witness evil in our lives,
And bear scars of pain and confusion before our eyes,
Habakkuk greatly reminds us to always hope in the Lord.
As He will penetrate grace upon us, like Judah, at all accords.

The Lamentations Over Sin

Jeremiah laments a course of destruction,
During Jerusalem's invasion and discriminations.
Inflicted from the Babylonians, Jerusalem felt weak,
Seeing nothing but pain that they could not speak.

Jeremiah expresses his raw feelings
On Jerusalem during 586 BC.

Like the book of Job, Lamentations starts dim,
Detailing the effects of evil- devastating suffering.

Yet searching at the heart, one sees,
That this book is more than a tragedy.
It is a book that paints sin of the world,
To then detail the hope of the Lord.

Zephaniah's Message From God

Zephaniah the son of Cushi, was unique.
His message impacted Judah's good kings.
As Zephaniah grew up, he stayed steadfast,
In proclaiming the messages of God.

Whenever the people were going astray,
Zephaniah was able to highlight the right way.
Zephaniah's primary goal was to save God's people,
From sin and ungodliness resulting to evil.

Despite the struggle, Zephaniah endured.
Purifying the people to their very core.

Zephaniah's story reminds you and I
To reflect our life as it passes by.
Are we living for real or just a façade?
Do we still love God through the pain?
Despite our human weakness, Zephaniah writes,
That God restores and fills us with His Might.

Haggai's Redirection For Future Blessing

Haggai was a prophet more than 70 years old,
And had seen Jerusalem's destruction unfold.
From their temple and exile in 586 BC,
The people were vulnerable and unhappy.

Haggai redirected the Jews to finish God's temple,
Fortunately, the Jews were receptive, not resentful.
Haggai's passion and zeal led the Jews to be victorious,
And showered with God's future blessings- so glorious.

Malachi's Call To Bring Israel Back

After returning from Babylon after 70 years,
God's love for His people was hard to believe.
Malachi came along to open their eyes,
And divert focus to their sinful lives.

Malachi hoped to create change.
So the people could return to God again.
Their return was accounted by repenting deeds,
So God could renew His covenant with ease.

Throughout the history books, page by page,
Israel's sin has always prompted God's grace.
The cycle of close to God, to unfaithful the next
Testifies human weakness being a process.
Yet through our struggles, tight as a rope.
As Malachi testifies here, we all have hope.
The God who extended His mercy to the Israelites.
Is the same God who lavishes His love time after time.

Jonah's Journey to See

There once lived a man named Jonah the prophet..
A prophet that was assigned by the Lord to preach at Nineveh,
As the people sinned and only a prophet could stop it.
But Jonah was stubborn and rejected God's call to minister.

Instead, Jonah decided to hide from God and aboard a ship.
A ship that would take him off opposite Ninevah, to Tarshish.
Upon boarding the ship, he falsely felt safe and happy.
Assuming that God would not notice or even be angry.

Little did Jonah know that God who sees all, saw.
And that God would not let him easily go.
So by the first night , the ship was caught in a storm.
And Jonah took it as a sign from God, but felt torn.
Not long after, Jonah got the nerve to ask,
All the sailors to through him in the sea at last.

Right after they threw Jonah, the fierce storm stopped.
And Jonah was swallowed by a whale on top.
One cannot imagine how he felt and handled.
The situation of being trapped inside a sea mammal.
Yet, Jonah was clever and choose to pray.

He prayed: "Lord how long shall I cry out to You?
In the belly of this whale, I promise to,
Preach to the Ninevites and put aside my pride.
I pray You forgive me, dear Lord, please hear my cry".

God the all-merciful, slow to anger and quick to forgive,
Accepted and heard Jonah's prayer to live.
By the command of God, the whale vomited him away,
At the shore of Ninevah, where Jonah would stay.

Jonah took this opportunity to learn to be brave.
And to help the Ninevites to willingly change.
Successfully Jonah was able to save,
The Ninevites and their city from perishing away.

However, Jonah was oddly apathetic on this result,
Accusing God for being too easy on humans and too soft.
God taught Jonah a lesson through a plant that gave him shade.
A plant that God made to speedily wither away.
Jonah was devastated and had a rant for this plant that died.

God reminded him of his selfishness and pride.
For in God's eyes, a human's salvation is worth more than a plant.
Jonah was humbled again at the memory of his superficial rant.

Indeed, Jonah finally learnt that God desires everyone to be saved,
And that we're called to lead others humbly in God's way.

Introduction to The Song of The Bow (Ref: 2 Samuel, Chapter 1)

For the Israelite people, overall,
David showed sorrow for Saul.
David's sorrow was sincere
And deeply felt by all.

David even crafted a song to express his sadness
Proving he was not one to hold a hatred.
Even when Saul greatly wronged him,
Leaving him weak and desolated.

Eventually David recovered from his grief,
He took on his throne,
Travelled abroad- beginning to speak.

The days following, David had a visitor.
It was a young man who looked sinister.
That very man, later confessed.
Revealing a confession:
He killed Saul,
But, at Saul's own request.

Then David asked the young man
"How could you, an Amalekite, accept?"

This question made the Amalekite very tense.
So, David decided to take revenge.

After that, David sent out the following command:
"Kill this man now,
For his actions are worthy of death".

Heeding To Hebron (Ref: 2 Samuel, Chapter 2)

In this time, David was still in Ziklag,
A territory for the Philistines to attack.
Interestingly, David left the land of Israel, to be there.
In fact, David ended up staying longer,
Due to his great discouragement and despair.

By the time David at last, felt restored,
He was ready to return to Israel,
His homeland, and place of the Lord.

David wanted more than God's blessing on his plans.
He wanted to be right in the middle of God's hands.

With a heart after God, God in return was faithful,
Making David keen to ask for guidance and peace
For the land of Israel.
Indeed, God elevated David
Whenever he was humbly on his knees.
Day by day, David did not seize the throne.
And as the elders of Judah approached him,
He always gave glory to God alone.

David also showed appropriate gratitude to his men,
Particularly the ones who honoured Saul and Jonathan.

David fostered more brave men to secure,
And advance his kingdom from anything impure.

Abner is revealed as Saul's cousin
A man of dignity
And a chief army commander.
So, as Abner meets David,
They both have friendly banter.

Later as the chapter foretells,
Abner makes Ishbosheth king.

For two years, David allowed Ishbosheth to reign,
Showcasing David's remarkable patience,
Longsuffering and resilience in pain.

Despite David's efforts of peace,
A man named Asahel, fought for David's kingship and seat.
Asahel was too single-minded and intense,
Leading to Abner killing him, in self-defence.

When Asahel's brother- Joab, found out on this occurrence.
He sought bloody revenge- but with a purpose.
Abner and Ishbosheth's army, lost three-hundred and sixty men
This was a large number,
Compared to the twenty fallen soldiers- all King David's men.

Undoubtedly, the house of Saul and the house of David,
Were destined to fail in getting along fully.

There could be no real peace,
Indeed, the ceasefire attempted to stop further wars.
The ceasefire only made things worse- for all.

Abner's Murder (Ref: 2 Samuel, Chapter 3)

During David's seven-year reign in Hebron
His six different wives gave birth to six sons.
This exposed David going against God's command,
By marrying more than just one woman.

Accordingly, David reaped the sin's penalty
Yet, God still showed David mercy.

Ishbosheth accuses Abner of misconduct with a royal concubine,
A concubine of Saul- when Saul was still alive.
Hence, this led to controversy on Abner being disloyal,
And inconsiderate for Saul's previous kingship and toil.

David appreciated Abner's allegiance,
However, Abner did this for alternative reasons.

Amid more of Israel's controversies and lies,
David added to Michal, to his collection of wives.

Joab accused Abner of being a double agent,
In return, David pronounced a severe curse.
A curse against Joab, that is, and no one else.

David did not want his kingdom established by violence.
For David still believed in the power of guidance,
And of vengeance belonging to the Lord.

Rechab and Baanah (Ref: 2 Samuel, Chapter 4)

Ishbosheth showed weakness.
For he did not trust in God, but in men.
The outcome of Ishbosheth's choice to do this,

Was destruction, pain, and further confusion.
Henceforth, when Ishbosheth's weakness was shown.

Rechab and Baanah plotted to murder him,
Which they eventually did, while he was on his throne.

Rechab and Baanah thought David would be pleased.
Afterall Ishbosheth took David's rightful place as king.
However, David was greatly disturbed by the news.
And the gift of Ishbosheth's severed head, was refused.

Turning to David's life, Mephibosheth is introduced.
Mephibosheth being the son of David's former friend,
David ensures that Mephibosheth- a lame twelve-year-old,
Was equally, if not more respected, from all.

Glory to Yah (Ref: 2 Samuel, Chapter 5)

As 2 Samuel, Chapter four records,
Ishbosheth was murdered, by the sword.
So now the tribes of Israel turned to David,
For his leadership, loyalty, and motivation.

Due to David being an Israelite,
The elders of Israel received him- in full delight.
This was a significant outcome for David,
Especially when he lived previously among the Philistines.
Hence, it was a miracle that the Israelite people did embrace,
And treat David with no anger, fear, or hate.

All told, David reigned 40 years.
His 15 years of preparation,
Equipped him for blood, sweat and tears.

Jebusites were quick to mock David.
For Jerusalem was easily invaded.
Nevertheless, David took the stronghold of Zion.
This resulted in making Israel unified.

Alas, the Philistines, again, brought along their idols.
They thought that this would make them entitled.
But the Lord gave a sign that he would work in this battle.
The sign was the sound of marching on mulberry trees- "tattle".

Indeed, because David inquired and obeyed God equally,
The Philistines failed in the battle- giving Israel victory.

Though, David was by no means, an "overnight success"
This battle is another example, of God making David, the best.

The Ark In The City (Ref: 2 Samuel, Chapter 6)

David gathered so many of his best soldiers
As bringing the ark to Jerusalem, was important.
After the ark was provided and set on a cart.
David inquired of the Lord, from his heart.

The ark was designed to be carried,
Only by the Levites- who are unmarried.

David and all the house of Israel played music before the Lord.
They did not hold back on dancing and making a burnt sacrifice.
The dancing and music marked the momentous occasion:
The Ark's arrival to the people of Israel- God's chosen nation.

Michal- Saul's daughter, judged David openly.
This was because David danced nakedly.
Yet, God understood David's intention was right.
So, God made Michal barren, for the rest of her life.

Then the Israelites came to Nachon's threshing floor,
Where the chaff was laid to the core.
David wanted Israel to know the presence of the Lord.
While God showed up, but not in the way people adored.
He blew all the chaff away.
Urging the Israelites to pray.

Alas, Uzzah placed his hand-irreverently.
On God's ark covenant.
Resulting in God killing him- with no relent.

Eternal, Unconditional Covenant (Ref: 2 Samuel, Chapter 7)

King David dwelled in a house of cedar wood.
It was a beautiful home in the neighbourhood.
When he remembered the Ark of God being inside tent curtains,
He was troubled by the thought that he lived in a nicer house.

With the prophet Nathan, King David held a meeting to discuss,
The process of making God a glorious temple.
God at first seemed honoured, then quite surprised.
Yet, David would not delay his plan or compromise.

God promised King David that under his reign,
He would establish a secure Israel.
For God knew that he, being a godly shepherd before,
Would consider the welfare of his people- forevermore.

God finally revealed to King David a pledge.
A pledge that Solomon, would build him a temple instead.
As God's words were David's foundation.
He readily accepted this great revelation.

David's Wars (Ref: 2 Samuel, Chapter 8)

King David attacked and subdued the Philistines,
Before then taking the land: Metheg Ammah, by surprise.
All in all, under King David's leadership, God's people were free,
And able to take territory back, from their enemies.

As the Moabites mistreated King David's parents,
The Moabites were killed in full abhorrence.

Next, King David went to recover his territory:
At the River Euphrates, to the Syrian Kingdom.
Following this, David took hold of golden shields and décor;
All of which belonged to Hadadezer's servants before.

Indeed, David took what was the glory of the enemy,
To glorify the goodness and power of the Lord.
Toi then sent Joram- his son, to greet King David.
King David accepted Joram's gifts and dedication.

From Syria, Moab, Ammon, Amalek, and the Philistines,
King David could handle success as well as his demise.

This chapter of victory, blessing, and prosperity,
Showcased King David's self-control and trust in God,
During the events of joy and misery.

David's Kindness (Ref: 2 Samuel, Chapter 9)

As King David remembered his covenant with Jonathan,
He was motivated to honour his descendants, for him.
King David pondered on how he could show kindness.
Hence, when he discovered Mephibosheth was Jonathan's son,
He made sure he was given prestige- respected by everyone.

When King David arrived, Mephibosheth fell on his face.
This was a custom for revering visitors at his place.

King David gave Mephibosheth a reason to not fear.
He promised a life filled with protection and cheer.

Although Mephibosheth did not feel worthy of such generosity,
King David restored Mephibosheth's land rights and family.

King David's promise to Mephibosheth was astounding.
After all, this 'dead dog', now accessed King David's housing.

Dwelling in King David's palace, Mephibosheth was blessed,
For King David continuously gave him honour, above and beyond the rest.

A War And A Defeat (Ref: 2 Samuel, Chapter 10)

King David continues his kindness mission.
Sending off servants with full permission.
The servants were assigned to comfort King Hanun
This Pagan King who was related to Saul, and that lost his father,
Allowed King David's servants to be mistreated- like no other.

When King David received back his servants in a terrible state,
He sent Joab and all the army of the mighty men.
All of which fought against King Hanun,
Seizing his servants' revenge.

The result was glorious:
King Hanun's Syrian soldiers became dead,
And before King David's soldiers,
The surviving Syrians fled.

Reign In Jerusalem (Ref: 2 Samuel, Chapter 11)

In the spring of the year, the kings went out to battle:
King David sent Joab for the battle- in place of him.
He did this to stay in Jerusalem.

While King David remained in his Kingdom, safe as can be.
He paced back and forth- he could not fall asleep.
Wide awake from the lack of sleep
King David saw a woman bathing.

As King David could not control his eyes.
His values soon became compromised.
Before he could refuse it, he inquired of the woman's name.
And what started as an inquiry of identity,
Developed to King David committing infidelity.

In taking Bathsheba, King David sinned against Uriah's name.
So, he quietly sent his messengers, to return her safe.

King David attempts to cover his sin of impurity.
He tests Uriah, only to find him being a man of integrity.

For the second attempt of a cover up, King David sends Uriah to fight.
Assigning Uriah to the frontline of the battle- in hopes he would die.
Unsurprisingly, Uriah did die.
Leaving David with some relief.
For now, he could marry Bathsheba,
And provide a reason for her pregnancy.
But little did David know,
That God above was watching- unpleased.

David's Sin (Ref: 2 Samuel, Chapter 12)

King David did not listen to the Holy Spirit's conviction.
Or even to his own conscience.
Thus, God sent the Prophet Nathan,
To make David finally listen.

Nathan applied the parable with alarming simplicity.
Nathan had to shock David into seeing his sin deeply.
The idea was that the man should have had pity on his neighbour
In the same way David should have had pity on Uriah.

From that day forward, God promised violence,
All of which, would run among David's descendants.

God spared King David with the penalty of death.
God had mercy on his shortcomings, at the very end.

Nevertheless, David's first child with Bathsheba, passed over.
This event left him and Bathsheba, with some trauma.
Yet, God again extends His mercy to them both.
And gives them another son- Solomon, for the throne.

Sick With Love (Ref: 2 Samuel, Chapter 13)

Amnon the son of King David
Was the first- born son from Ahinoam.
Amnon was spoiled and conceited,
As he was first in line, for Israel's throne.

Marriages between half-siblings was forbidden.
Yet, Amnon loved Tamar- his half- sister.
So, Amnon asked advice from Jonadab-his crafty cousin.
And this advice began a disastrous chain of events.

Amnon asked his father to assign Tamar to bring him cakes,
King David had no idea, that this visit would lead to rape.
Amnon had no real love for Tamar, only lust
For immediately after he committed the wrong,
He felt guilt, remorse, and disgust.

Alas, Tamar was a victim to Amnon's deception.
The terrible visit, left Tamar with no choice.
For Amnon had to redeem the situation.
Leaving Tamar- the Israelite princess, with no voice.

The only comfort Tamar received
Was from her brother Absalom.
Absalom's sympathy and grief for Tamar,
Soon transformed for hatred against Amnon,
And a hidden animosity.

Tamar did not bother to go to her father- King David,
For she knew he would excuse Amnon's behaviour.
However, to Tamar's full disbelief,
Her father became with grief.

Though two years went by, from that dreadful day.
Absalom did not stop plotting revenge at bay.
Therefore, when Absalom threw a Feast,

He hastened the day
And murdered Amnon- as he pleased.

David's Reign in Jerusalem (Ref: 2 Samuel, Chapter 14)

Joab the son of Zeruiah, had an idea.
An idea to make King David and his son, unite.
Hence, Joab brought a widow in tears,
In hopes she would soften David's heart, in time.

The widow confidently pleads her predicament,
A story of family estrangement,
A story King David could comprehend.
And at the end of the widow's plea,
David listens to her wisdom about reconciliation.

After this feeble widow of Tekoa ends her wisdom.
King David asks her if Joab prompted her to come.

Indeed, Joab hoped that reconciliation of father and son,
Would prevent an occurrence of a rebellion.

Absalom was a man of deep and sympathetic feeling.
These qualities made Israel happy and willing.
Absalom even memorialized his wronged sister Tamar.
He did this by naming his own daughter, after her.

When Absalom is refused by King David at first,
He, in frustration burnt Joab's fields.
This was an intentional outburst worked.
And Joab interceded on Absalom's behalf.

Finally, King David offered Absalom forgiveness.
He did not give proper resolution of his past mistakes.
So, because of no real repentance,
Absalom was left ignorant- and did not change.

Coup D'etat By Absalom (Ref: 2 Samuel, Chapter 15)

Absalom continues to steal Israel's hearts.
From his handsome appearance and charisma,
Absalom becomes trusted and popular.
Taking over his father's stamina.

Next, Absalom stirred up dissatisfaction
Within and around his father- King David's government.
Then, he campaigned across the land,
Fulfilling many promises.

Absalom projected he was a "man of the people".
For instance, he would not let others bow down to him,
Rather, he would lift them up,
Shake their hands and embrace them.

Absalom's cunning campaign worked.
So much so, that he became more popular.
As a result, people of Israel trusted his word,
Far more than of King David's.

Following this, under the guise of devotion,
Absalom committed treason in motion.

In the end, King David escapes
But only with the help of faithful friends.
The priests were loyal to David,
Even though it probably meant death for them.
Unmistakably, David continued to trust in God,
And not the ark of the covenant.

Sorrow And Regret (Ref: 2 Samuel, Chapter 16)

Ziba, the servant of Mephibosheth,
Whom King David had showed great kindness,

Worked to deceive David and break his trust,
With Mephibosheth- Jonathan's son.

Ziba succeeded in the deception.
David believed his word- with no question.
As a result, Ziba's façade of loyalty, is rewarded.
Leaving Mephibosheth punished with full reproof.

Enter in Shimei- a distant relative of former King Saul,
Curses King David and threatens his Kingdom, on a whole.
King David receives this adversity with humility.
He did not try to shut Shimei at all.
Instead, he focused on God to comfort him,
And kept his peace, knowing God was in control.

After meditating on God's will,
King David sends Hushai back on a mission.
The mission was to spy on Absalom,
Until he was in full remission.

Hushai succeeded in spying
Along with providing Absalom bad advice.
As a result, Ahithophel told Absalom to take revenge.
Revenge by violating King David's women, once again.

Unfortunate Soul (Ref: 2 Samuel, Chapter 17)

The advice from Ahithophel and of Hushai,
Were destructive and evil indeed.
Oh, how unfortunate for King David and his son,
To carry for each other, this animosity.

Hushai knew David could barely keep himself together,
So, he prayed that God would give David victory.
Next, Hushuai advises Absalom to raise a huge army,
To win David more time to attack the enemy.

Under Hushai's plan, Absalom was destined to die.
And as a result, Ahithophel committed suicide.

Absalom's Pillar (Ref: 2 Samuel, Chapter 18)

David organized his army.
He set them into three divisions- equally.
Some were under commander Joab,
Some were under commander Abishai
And some were under commander Ittai the Gittite.

King David knew how to submit to others' wisdom.
He did not give up leadership; but loved to assign captains.

The experienced leadership of David,
Along with his captains too,
Was the reason for their overwhelming victory.

Joab did not hesitate to strike Absalom, from the start.
For Joab had King David's best interest, at heart.

Without saying it directly,
The Cushite informed King David on Absalom's death.
And to everyone's surprise,
David broke down and wept.

Kingdom Restoration (Ref: 2 Samuel, Chapter 19)

King David continued to mourn for some time.
The extended mourning made Joab lose his mind.
For Joab could hardly understand,
Why David missed his son- despite the predicament.

King David's excessive sorrow also made,
His loyal friends feel very ashamed.
So, Joab rebuked him- calling him self-centred.
Hence, prompting him to serious repentance.

Following this, King David sends forth,
Negotiators to the tribes of Israel.
The efforts of both Zadok and Abiathar, do well.
Leaving David to be welcomed back again- in Israel.

King David shows forgiveness to Shimei.
Shimei in return, is humble and contrite.
Following King David's forgiveness streak,
Mephibosheth willingly gave Ziba his property.

Following, David shows appreciation to Barzillai.
For Barzillai brought essential help to him before.
In gratitude, David offered him honour and supplies.
Barzillai respectfully declined this kindness,
But, eventually accepted it on behalf of his son.

Despite the goodness spreading like confetti,
This could not stop the ten northern tribes feeling jealousy.
And because of the competitive nature of these tribes, ,
A civil war broke out before King David's eyes.

Continuation Of Judah (Ref: 2 Samuel, Chapter 20)

After Absalom's failed try of rebellion,
Sheba took advantage of King David's authority.
Hence, Sheba succeeded in stirring up the ten northern tribes,
Thereby causing King David's kingdom to divide.

The desertion of the ten tribes was distressing,
But the loyalty of the men of Judah was wonderful.

Tired of waiting, King David sends Joab- his royal commander and chief
Who then leads the royal servants to battle- and claim victory.

Using deception, Joab kills Amasa,
And defeats Sheba in one accord.

Indeed, Joab was a practical man.
So, King David kept allowing Joab to command.

The greatness of King David's kingdom was not on him alone,
But rather God, and the people like Joab,
All of which, endorsed his authority on the throne.

Avenging The Gibeonites (Ref: 2 Samuel, Chapter 21)

From wars, bad people, and terrible famines,
King David wisely sought God, in all these challenges.

After three years of famine, King David initiated a tenacity.
The tenacity would foster peace with the Gibeonites-a previous enemy.
For David felt that if the Gibeonites could bless Israel again,
Then God's chastening of Israel, would come to an end.

The Gibeonites only asked for justice against Saul.
So, King David made sure the Gibeonites, were given rights.

Except for Mephibosheth alone,
Seven male descendants of Saul were forlorn.
This made the Gibeonites hold their peace.
Especially since they executed the seven men, publicly.

Rizpah – the mother of two of the seven men executed,
Held a vigil over the bodies, until the late rains colluded.
The coming of rain showed that the famine had subsided.
Thereby indicating that justice, was finally satisfied.

King David also gave these seven, a public burial,
Together with the remains of Saul and Jonathan.

As the years went on, King David became unable to fight.
Hence, Sibbechai, Elhanan and Jonathan, helped David take charge.
Accordingly, Israel's enemy: **four giants**, were killed at last.

Even when King David grew faint in battle,
God continuously protected him from harm.
Nevertheless, as the battle ended,
He accepted that his 'warrior season', had passed.

A Sticky Situation (Ref: 2 Samuel, Chapter 22)

The psalm appears almost as David's final words.
Hence, it is a summary of thanksgiving for God's good works.
Each title was meaningful to David.
Particularly because God remained faithful.

Prayer and praise for King David was that easy.
He cried out to God and wrote out his heart completely.
Indeed, King David pictured the LORD coming to meet his needs.
Coming with glory, mercy, and full speed.

King David always knew that God would defend,
Him and his Kingdom, from all ends.

King David gave every victory credit to God's hand.
Undeniably, he carried a zeal, to follow God's command.

Every plea for deliverance was rooted in his closeness to God.
God, for King David was much more than a desire to survive.
Rather, God, for King David, was a reason, to be alive.

Even when King David sinned by committing adultery,
God had compassion on him and Bathsheba,
As King David had compassion, to the former king: Saul.
Clearly, King David's wise actions,
Granted him and Bathsheba mercy, once and for all.

King David continued to endeavour for perfection.
Such an endeavour took considerable to maintain.
Thus, at times, King David received God's glory and fame,
And, other times, he received God's blunt correction.

When God met King David's need, He brought security.
God gave him power, strength, and purity.

King David relished the place of victory he had in the LORD.
He was not hesitant to ever proclaim it.
Even on the throne, King David believed God sustained him.
Truly, this former shepherd boy,
Never forgot where he came from.

The Annointed God Of Jacob (Ref: 2 Samuel, Chapter 23)

Ruling his people justly and unstained by corrupts.
King David reaches the zenith of his power,
Making the ark of God's covenant
Remaining safe and secure.

The sons of Belial are introduced as worthless and insecure.
The sons were admitted to test King David,
And challenge his leadership and faith- to the core.

A list is admitted at King David's throne.
The list contained sixteen relatives,
Some of which were from the line of King David,
And some from the line of former King Saul.

Bethlehem supplies water by an aqueduct.
Leaving the wells to close the town, around about.

King David retracts a burning fever,
And becomes further depressed when he learns,
That Abishai committed exploitation,
By making irreverent leaders in King David's house.

God's Invisible Hand (Ref: 2 Samuel, Chapter 24)

It was up to God to command a counting of the Israelites.
Alas, King David's heart, was moved by Satan's vice.

Hence, King David numbered the people,
From the soldiers, army captains, to the simple man.
King David's numbering was disobedience of God's orders.
And tested God's invisible hand.

Joab, who was never afraid to speak the veracity,
Reprimanded King David in full normality.

It took almost 10 months to complete the numerical census.
The results showed that there were 1,300,000 fighting men.
This large number of men counted among the twelve tribes,
Gave King David a false sense of security and pride.

God used King David's sin and chastised him accordingly.
Therefore, King David's Kingdom endured three days of plague.

The devastating plague struck many, in such a short period of time.
Yet, King David preferred falling into the hands of God's mercies,
Rather than having to fight his enemies, all the time.

To please God again, King David purchased land,
But little did he know,
That this land, according to God's plan,
Would be the future temple,
For the Israelites to worship in and go.

Reign of Solomon
(Ref: 1 Kings, Chapter 1)

King David was old and advanced in age.
So much so, that he began to wonder 'Who will prevail?'
Being seventy years old currently,
He knew his kingship had ended his prime.

From the moral clouds from his choices of wives.
He was tangled in lust, for his concubines.
To add, with a family history of treachery and homicide,
King David's kingdom needed a King- who'd be wise.

As the throne was not left for hereditary succession,
God had to determine the next new King.
First, as Adonijah violated a basic principle.
God refused to make him the King of His people.

Likewise, Amnon failed the Kingship test,
Leaving God, to refuse him as the next.
Alas, King David failed to discipline his sons in time.
Making God reject his sons, as next in line

Ironically, the sons didn't take the rejection lightly.
Adonijah, even decided to throw a party.
The party was a way for Adonijah to show off his 'goods':
From money, women, power, and killer good looks.

Zadok the priest, Nathan the Prophet and Benaiah,
Were the three prominent leaders, who rejected Adonijah.
After equal refusals to crown Adonijah as king and ruler,
Adonijah's true wickedness, flashed all over.
In accordance to King David's promise to Bathsheba,
Solomon was chosen by God, as King and leader.
Following this, Nathan the prophet came in to stay,
To provide Solomon support, during his royal reign.

In support, Benaiah, made a pious wish, in name,
For it involved Solomon exceeding in his reign.
Indeed, this wish was fulfilled to the principle.
But on a material level- not eternal or spiritual.

The city was in uproar, as Solomon was crowned King,
Feasts, music and dancing, decorated Israel's streets.
At first Adonijah was jealous all round,
But when Solomon showed him mercy,
Adonijah could only show gratitude,
And even support, for Solomon's run of the town.

Glory To God (Ref: 1 Kings, Chapter 2)

Knowing that he would soon pass from this life,
King David gave final charge to Solomon, to stay upright.
King David knew that Solomon needed strength and bravery,
To handle all his responsibilities successfully.

King David also instructed Solomon to always obey God,
For he knew too well what would happen- if Solomon defied.
Truly, King David wanted Solomon to keep the throne of Israel,
And to exhort justice to all, before surrendering to the grave.

So, to follow through King David's legacy.
Solomon showed kindness to the sons of Barzillai.
On top of giving an allowance of food, attire, and currency,
King Solomon invited the sons of Barzillai for dinner.

King Solomon sat on the throne of his late father- David.
Fulfilling his vows, obeying God's word- keeping his status.
He was even zealous to give justice to Adonijah,
As he understood the situation perfectly.

To begin with, Adonijah wanted to attempt, yet again,
To steal Solomon's kingdom- and make himself the King instead.
Therefore, King Solomon had no other preference,
But to put Adonijah to death for his aggression.

The same death fate came for Abiathar,
As he supported the unlawful Adonijah.
Yet, before Abiathar's life was put to end,
King Solomon showed him mercy- totally unplanned.
Moreover, to fulfil the word of the Lord, concerning the house of Eli
King Solomon eradicated Abiathar's status- as a practising priest.

Alas, another supported of Adonijah- Joab, was not so lucky.
Thus, King Solomon ordered Joab's execution - right at the altar.
In line with God's promise of peace to David and his descendants.
King Solomon extended mercies to Shimei, who later abused it.
Nevertheless, King Solomon's throne remained secure,
Strong, yet in full submission, to God's fate.

Great Wisdom (Ref: 1 Kings, Chapter 3)

After marrying the Pharaoh's daughter,
King Solomon made a treaty that would prosper.
Both Egypt and Israel just the equivalent.
So, the people of Israel remained to God- observant.

Under the law of Moses, the people of Israel sacrificed,
Bulls, Goats, and all acceptable offerings,
On the altars at the "High places".
Untouched by the practise of idolatry.

As King Solomon loved the Lord with all his heart,
He constructed a temple, for future sacrifice rituals, to take part.
Following the construction of the temple, King Solomon also sacrificed,
A total of one thousand burnt offerings- a truly grotesque amount.

Besides demonstrating his great wealth and heart, through and through.
King Solomon went to sacrifice, at the great high place of Gibeon, too.
What made it different at Gibeon, was that the tabernacle was around,
Even though the ark of the covenant was Jerusalem bound.

The Lord appeared to Solomon in a wonderous dream.
This remarkable visitation challenged Solomon's fear.
God offered Solomon whatever he wanted,
As God wanted to work something in Solomon, through his response.

Before responding, Solomon remembered God's mercies and truths,
Towards his father David, to now himself, and the Israel people, too.
Upon this beautiful reflection, Solomon knew exactly what he would do.
So, he asked in full humility, for the gift of wisdom, during his mighty rule.

As King Solomon asked for more than things,
God answered his request for wisdom, readily.
Clearly, King Solomon understood his leadership role,
A role to lead, serve God and the people of Israel.

From judging the people, on good and evil,
King Solomon used discernment to make all equal.

From poor to the rich, all people were treated fair,
King Solomon's speeches came naturally, as breathing air.

As King Solomon's speeches also pleased the Lord,
He was blessed with many things he did not ask for.
From fame, wealth, and power above one's wildest dreams.
King Solomon followed the Lord's words, in everything.

An example of King Solomon's glorious reign,
Was when two women- harlots came to complain.
They had a word against one another,
One lying about a newborn child- stating they were the "mother".
Fortunately, King Solomon's wisdom helped settle the dispute.
And the true parental relationship of the newborn child, was proved.

As all of Israel heard of the wise decision, King Solomon had made.
The people were more hesitant, to ever break his laws, or disobey.

United Kingdom (Ref: 1 Kings, Chapter 4)

Just as the story of the harlots contending over the newborn child,
King Solomon's extended wisdom so subtle and mild.
From selecting, and empowering, official leaders, priests, and scribes,
The workload was evenly distributed to always protect Israel.

Twelve governors were responsible for taxation in their districts.
Which thereby ran on mountains, lands, and all the far regions.
As each district made a provision once a month, each year,
King Solomon's reign kept the Kingdom in reverent fear.

From reigning over Egypt's Nile River, to the land of the Philistines,
Israel experienced neighbourly peace- unlike in King David's time.
With God's providence, the kingdom thrived continually
Yet, King Solomon was vulnerable to the sin of gluttony.

In fact, each day, he, his entire household, and royal court,
Would devour ten fatted oxen, and one hundred sheep, in one accord.

What is more, thirty kors of flour, equivalent to 220 litres in size,
Would be delivered each day to make bread and sweet delights.

Indeed 'each man was under his vine and fig tree",
In other words, the people of Israel had peace and prosperity.
With King Solomon's cavalry and chariots- 40,000 in total,
This vast amount of assets kept Israel safe from trouble.

Each man in the kingdom were given charge,
A charge to fulfil their duty and keep Israel from harm.
Such wisdom from King Solomon, was blessed from Lord,
Thereby growing his fame in all surrounding nations abroad.

The Israelites and surrounding nations, coined him wiser than all,
Then Ethan the Ezrahite and Heman, the author of the 88th Psalm.
King Solomon spoke three thousand proverbs, enough to make a book.
And his songs were one thousand and five in total- it was just as good.

Temple Work (Ref: 1 Kings, Chapter 5)

As Hiram had always loved King David, and supported his reign,
He willingly helped King Solomon, even more, just the same.
Although not an Israelite, Hiram heard all spiritual topics and things,
And assisted King Solomon's construction of glorious buildings.

From towers, statues, and the Lord's temple of course,
The Lord put King Solomon's enemies, under his feet's soles.
So, there were no adversaries or evil occurrences,
After all, King Solomon kept his vow to create the Lord a temple.

King Solomon didn't build a temple for a name,
But for the Israelites to pray to the Lord in reverence- again.
Hence, the temple was built from cedar trees of Lebanon,
Excellent timber that would grow stronger, each month.

In reward for Hiram being a respectable man,
Hiram and his household were granted food, as payment.
Undoubtedly, King Solomon had a godly influence on Hiram,
As his kindness to Hiram, brought peace between Israel and Lebanon:
An outcome, undoubtedly blessed, by the good Lord alone.

A huge labour force of thirty thousand men,
Kept the temple construction protected, on every end.
King Solomon delegated every Israelite a role,
To maintain balance of the workload for all.

Adoniram oversaw the entire labour force.
Seventy thousand carried burdens, and eighty thousand quarried costly stone.
Three thousand three hundred worked as chiefs.
To administer the building of the Lord's temple.

The Lord's temple truly had quality materials
Keeping it fully spec and clean.
From the hidden foundation stones to the jewels
There was no material that could not be seen.
And unfortunately, the temple grew the envy of some:
The Gebalities people- on the coast of the Mediterranean Sea.

Long -Awaited Temple of The Lord (Ref: 1 Kings, Chapter 6)

In the four hundred and eightieth year,
King Solomon began ear by ear,
Building the Lord's wonderful house of prayer,
A sight for all to stop and stare.

The measurements of the Lord's house, were as follows:
Sixty cubits on twenty and thirty; not large as ancient temples go.

Yet, the glory of the Lord's temple, was not in its' size,
But rather, in the peace it brought to the people inside.

Chamber rooms were also built adjacent to the temple,
With the same stones used to build the temple.
On top of that, panelled beams, and boards of cedar, were created,
Giving off a finely finished look – for the three storied, side chambers.

The Lord made a conditional promise to King Solomon and his descendants,
A promise of blessing, in exchange for King Solomon's obedience and repentance.

After seven years of building, and carving the temple, carefully.
The Lord's temple was a spectacular sight for all to see.

Solomon's Palace and Furnishings (Ref: 1 Kings, Chapter 7)

King Solomon took thirteen years to build his house.
On top of richly panelled walls,
The cedar wood was used.
Making his house truly magnificent, inside, and out.

It was clear that the temple's architectural features,
Were used in the building of King Solomon's house.
Huram, a talented craftsman, being half Israeli and half Gentile
Was hired by King Solomon, to do artistic designs.

Without further ado, Huram cast two bronze pillars,
The first pillar was named after the prophet Jachin,
Leaving the second being named Boaz- a prophet name too.

After setting up the noteworthy pillars,
Huram set out to make ten lavers
With forty baths, each five meters wide.

And these baths were used,
For the temple's ceremonial washings inside.

Ten tables of showbread were placed on a gold table,
With a total of ten cards, shovels, bowls, and other utensils.
On top of this, more furnishings that former King- David, had dedicated,
Were included to rightly worship, God the Father and Creator.

The Temple's Dedication (Ref: 1 Kings, Chapter 8)

King Solomon assembled the elders of Israel,
Into devised heads of the twelve tribes.
Each head of the tribe was called 'chief father in charge'
And rightly so, for each head was responsible in large.

As the ark of the convent, was still not in the temple,
King Solomon had to assign the priests for help.
So, the priests took up the ark of the covenant carefully,
And elevated in the temple for Israel to witness and see.

As all the holy furnishings were now in the tabernacle- ready,
The priests sacrificed sheep and oxen – on behalf of many.
These sacrifices were an expectation to honour and praise God;
Hence, as a result the Kingdom was protected from enemy's harm.

Apart from two tablets of stone which Moses put at Horeb,
The ark of covenant contained nothing else inside.
At an earlier point in Israel's history, there were three items.
The golden pot that had manna, and priest Aaron's rod.
No one knows 'til this day, what happened to the golden pot and rod,
All we know is that the two tablets remained- by God's grace.

The Lord made a covenant with the children of Israel,
To remind them of their deliverance from slavery- in Egypt.

And a cloud filled up the Lord's house in one accord,
To signify the shining radiance of the Lord.

Whenever the cloud appeared before the priests' eyes,
The priests stopped ministering until it disappeared inside.
This is because the cloud signified God's presence,
Making it a very breathtaking sight- and equally intense.

King Solomon sensed the presence of the cloud, representing the Lord,
So, he spoke pure words of praise and prayer from the heart.
Again, King Solomon pressed on the remembrance of Exodus,
Which in turn, kept the Israelites in a state of repentance.

King Solomon exclusively assigned the High Priest's descendants,
To dedicate and influence the Israelites' path to repentance.
The High Priest's descendants would also spread out their hands toward Heaven,
To demonstrate surrender, openness, and ready reception.

King Solomon recognised that God was completely unique,
So, he never ceased to thank and praised God for all his successes,
Indeed, as he would boldly and reverently call on God for everything.
God kept protecting him and the Israelites; and forgave their transgressions.

King Solomon knew that God was far too great to be restricted to the temple,
So, he would fearlessly supplicate to God, with no pretention.
As a result, God would always incline His ear to him- for the sake of the Kingdom.
And the people of Israel experienced answered prayers, and whole lotta forgiveness.

On the temple grounds, oaths were also authorised.
To help settle personal issues and disputes of all kinds.

King Solomon knew that the hidden intentions of men, were hard to see,
Therefore, he requested God to inspire him to judge everyone – and fairly.

Many times, in history when Israel strayed away from God freely,
They would suffer merciless defeats from their enemy,
God truly kept His Word of protecting and blessing when the people were humble,
Grateful to God for his mercies and loving Him with a pure heart- no grumble.

God truly had a good response to the Israelites' repentance,
He forgave and restored their loss,
In exchange for a faith unshaken.
King Solomon recognised and pleaded with God.
From his own chambers and in the temple- all the time,
As a result, God blessed the Kingdom,
And continued to save it from demise.

Moreover, concerning a foreigner, God intended for all nations to pray.
In the glorious temple, with no fear or dismay.
So, the Gentiles were permitted to join the people of Israel,
In prayer and dedication to God- unprevailed.

King Solomon prayed with the idea that God should answer the prayers:
Prayers for victory in every foreign military mission, and every foreign land.
The principle of the inevitable- sin happening, was not a blanket notion at all,
For King Solomon knew that humans were prone to make mistakes- and fall.

After sacrificing twenty-two thousand bulls and one hundred and twenty thousand sheep.

King Solomon rest assured that God answered his prayers- and would keep listening.
At that same time, King Solomon held a glorious feast,
To once again, celebrate God's gifts of goodness, and peace.

Trades and Dominion (Ref: 1 Kings, Chapter 9)

When King Solomon had finished building the house of the Lord,
He had to deal with the issues of life in the Kingdom.
The Lord appeared to King Solomon for the second time.
This special appearance reassured that his prayers weren't denied.

The building of the house of the Lord, was Solomon's work.
Leaving God alone, expected to bless and hallow it.
God's answer to King Solomon's previous prayer, had a condition:
For Solomon to expect blessing during his reign if he committed.

So, King Solomon and his descendants, made sure to do the right thing,
To keep the blessing and protection from the Lord, remaining within.
The positive promise of God, was followed by another negative one,
Then God filled the temple with His glorious presence- encouraging everyone.

Israel became the proverb that left everyone in astonishment.
At the hard work of God, and the Israelite people's covenant.
In return for Hiram- the King of Tyre, supplying cedar, cypress, and gold,
King Solomon gave Hiram, twenty cities in Galilee, to rule and own.

As a result of King Solomon trading Israel's land, the labour force grew.
Prompting King Solomon to conduct massive building projects too.
He built the Milo- a prominent fortress near the temple and palace.
Then he continued to fortify three cities: Hazor, Megiddo and Gezer.

The Amorites, Hittites, Perizzites, Hivites and Jebusite people remaining outside;

Were assigned by King Solomon, to oversee remnants of the Canaanite tribes.
Three times a year, King Solomon offered burnt and peace offerings on the altar,
Following this, he would initiate Israelite representatives to go to Ophir.
Ophir was a Southern Arabia place and great enterprise;
Hence, a total of four hundred and twenty talents of gold, was for King Solomon, acquired.

The Gift of Wisdom (Ref: 1 Kings, Chapter 10)

The Queen of Sheba, also known as Sabea,
Came from a wealthy kingdom and geography.
Her Kingdom had gold, spices, and precious woods,
Which impressed King Solomon- more than he should.

Equally, the Queen of Sheba was also impressed,
By King Solomon's wisdom, so she made a request.
She requested King Solomon to answer all her questions.
And in return, gifted him a great retinue- no objections.

When she came into King Solomon's Kingdom and house,
She was full of questions – quite difficult to put apart.
But, when she received the overwhelming wisdom of King Solomon,
She finally had a comforting peace in her heart.

As the Queen of Sheba left, she began to reiterate:
"I have not seen such wisdom and riches in my state,
You are truly a great king, who makes all happy and safe,
Indeed, blessed be the Lord your God, who made you king,
And hence provided you with a wonderful fate".

There never again came such abundance of spices given,
As from the Queen of Sheba, for King Solomon's kingdom.
On top of spices, she gave six hundred and sixty-six talents of gold,
A huge sum equivalent to nearly a billion dollars alone.

Apart from receiving travelling merchant goods,
King Solomon received a hundred large shields too.
The shields were made of gold- pretty, but with no substance.
Proving that King Solomon played the image of a 'warrior king'
For he had no experience, or warfare presence.

King Solomon gathered chariots, horses, and horsemen to the number:
A total of one thousand four hundred chariots,
With one thousand four hundred horses imported from Keyeh and Egypt,
And twelve thousand responsible horsemen.

Not one treasure of King Solomon, was other than gold.
Hence showing his tremendous wealth- from new to old.
Yet, King Solomon fell at times when he broke God's commands,
In importing goods from places other than Israel's lands.
Nevertheless, people from all ends of the Earth, still came to visit,
To see and hear King Solomon's God-given wisdom.

Divisive Kingdom to Be (Ref: 1 Kings, Chapter 11)

King Solomon loved foreign women- to many to hold,
All of which were Pagan- breaking God's laws.
God had commanded again, for no one to intermarry,
As for God, marriage is a sacrament- not a time to tarry.

Despite God's mercy and clear guidance, to do what is right.
Many people followed King Solomon's example- and defied.
Clearly, King Solomon's great wisdom, didn't apply to marriage.
For he had sensual fulfilments with seven hundred wives
And bad romances with three hundred concubines.

King Solomon set the tone of lust- leaving collateral damage.
For all the men of Israel, slowly lost reverence for marriage.
All the Pagan women in King Solomon's life, turned his heart away:
Away from God, following God's commands, and his will to pray.

King Solomon shows us that the blessing and power of God comes,
But only with obedience to God's commands and living in His truth.
Hence, it is of no surprise that King Solomon's unguarded heart,
Made him disloyal to God- destroying his reputation, through and through.

As the Lord became angry with King Solomon- and rightly so.
For King Solomon's sin was based on ingratitude and pride.
All of which wasted his great spiritual privilege,
Heritage, wisdom and blessing from God inside.

Hence, God planned to reprimand King Solomon in a certain way,
A way where his kingdom would be divided- teared away.
Indeed, as God promised King David that King Solomon would be safe,
God waited for King Solomon's death,
To finally initiate the kingdom's divisive fate.

King Solomon's reign was glorious but had some difficulties throughout.
From adversaries like from Hadad the Edomite, and Rezon the son of Eliadah.
To betrayal from former Israelite Jeroboam-the son of Nebat.
Israel was conquered by enemies from the North and South.

King Solomon sought to kill Jeroboam himself- due to feeling betrayed.
Hence proving King Solomon's slow decline of wisdom- each day.
God's word through Ahijah also proved to be true,
That King Solomon would reign over all Israel for forty years,
Before passing away, leaving a divisive kingdom too.

Rehoboam, Solomon's Foolish Advisor (Ref: 1 Kings, Chapter 12)

Rehoboam went to Shechem under the assumption that he'd be king,
This was a logical assumption, for he continued the Davidic dynasty.

But when Jeroboam- the son of Nebat, heard the news.
He decided to take part of the Israelite elders' group.

King Solomon's passing, left a heavy taxation,
So, Rehoboam consulted with the elders- on welfare for the nation.
After consulting with the elders about taxes and burdensome services,
Rehoboam asked the young men for their unique opinion and advice.

The young men were quite irrational and emotionally driven,
Yet, Rehoboam rejected the elders' advice, and chose to not listen.
As a result, the young men who knew Rehoboam from their youth,
Had their advice received and formalised it as the truth.

Rehoboam's foolishness made Israel reject not only him,
But all the descendants of King David- the greatest king.
Following the stoning of Adoram- King Rehoboam's chief tax collector,
A full-blown rebellion against the kingdom, was finally on the radar.

From this point in history of Israel, the twelve tribes took the rebellion seriously,
So, when Israel heard that Jeroboam had come back, they sent for him;
Before calling him to the congregation and making him king.
This event proved the rebellion was dangerously rising.

Despite the prophecy of Ahijah sounding untrue,
The rebellion in Israel, just grew and grew.
Before anyone could blink, Jeroboam built a capital city- which he called Shechem.
To keep his unlawful ruling and rebellion, strong in every end.

The divided kingdom continued under the law of the prophet- Moses,
Yet, Jeroboam kept failing to comply to the covenant.
Instead, Jeroboam appealed to his natural desire for ease.

Little did he know that God was not pleased.

Jeroboam only cared about pleasing people and showing power,
He cared to be seen as a man of authority and valour.
As a result, Jeroboam set the tone of sin- worshipping false gods:
Albeit these were pagan idols, and golden shrines.

Jeroboam stands as a negative example for us all,
On the consequences of creating your own religion,
Betraying God before later forgetting Him altogether,
And blindly leading vulnerable others, to fall.

The Man of God From Judah (Ref: 1 Kings, Chapter 13)

This is a sad commentary on the spiritual state,
Of Jeroboam's kingdom and future fate.
A man of God went from Judah to Bethel:
Preaching that there were no qualified messengers,
Not one, within the northern kingdom of Israel.

Following this bad revelation,
A young boy- Josiah by name.
Was prophesied to be born,
From the house of King David.

Additionally, the prophecy detailed sacrifice,
To be always practised on the high places by the priests.
This was another remarkable prophecy,
Which was fulfilled 340 years later- precisely.

On the same day, the prophet shared another sign,
A sign that the altar would split, with ashes poured inside.
Such a sign would convincingly rebuke,
The Israelites for worshipping idols besides God too.

Upon hearing these terrible lists of prophecies,
King Jeroboam cried: "Arrest this man immediately".
Indeed, Jeroboam sought to silence, rather than respond,
To the prophecies relayed from this man of God.

As a result, this implicit invitation to repentance,
Was not adhered, leaving Israel in the wrong direction.

With full nerve, King Jeroboam was about to strike,
The man of God in full despite.
But by the grace of God, his hand withered right away.
And he could harm the man of God- leaving him ashamed.

"Please entreat the favour of the LORD", King Jeroboam pleaded.
Fortunately, the man of God, forgave and retreated.
And Jeroboam was given a great grace and compassion
From the man of God, and God- who answered his prayer.

Given the circumstances, Jeroboam quickly embraced
The man of God as a friend, that he could not replace.
Despite Jeroboam inviting him to break bread as a reward,
The man of God refused the invitation- staying faithful to the Lord.

Alas, the man of God was later conned by
A false prophet of Bethel, who spread a lie.
The lie was that God permitted the man of God to accept,
The invitation from Jeroboam- with no regrets.

God promised great judgment against his defiance.
Indeed, he failed this hard test, by believing in the lies.
He should have kept the commandment that the Lord had produced
Rather than taking a false prophet's word, without further ado.

God judged the man of God from Judah, far more strictly
As a lesson, to ever again heed to a lying prophecy.

Not long after this judgement of his corpse burial, was made.
A lion met him on the road and killed him in haste.

Indeed, this lion was on a special mission of judgment from God
And seemed to be more obedient than the man of God ever was.

Jeroboam And Rehoboam's End (Ref: 1 Kings, Chapter 14)

At that time Abijah- Jeroboam's son, became crook,
Prompting him to seek a prophet to help and look.
In time of need, Jeroboam would turn back to the true God,
For his heart knew that idols could not help him at all.

Sure, Jeroboam was a king, but even kings have worry.
From disguising himself to see a fortune teller- in a hurry.
The woman's disguise and Ahijah's blindness didn't matter,
Because God told Ahijah the truth of the matter.

From this, the wife of Jeroboam learned two things:
First, to brace herself for the bad news to be said
Second, that Ahijah's message was truly God-sent.
So, although Saul was a bad man, Jeroboam was far worse.
Hence, Jeroboam was angry to be coined as a 'bad king'.

Jeroboam felt that God cast him behind His back,
As disasters happened in Jeroboam's house.
Indeed, Jeroboam wasted God's promises and mercies,
Due to his unbelief, lust, and many idolatries.

Jeroboam sent his wife to discover the fate of their son,
A fate being that their son would die- in front of everyone.
Yet, their son's death would be a demonstration of God's mercy,
An event for Jeroboam to try repentance and humility.

After three hundred years later, the Lord's command was fulfilled
A command for the uproot of Israel and scattered from the hills.
Indeed, God knew that the root of Jeroboam's apostasy,
Would eventually result to bitter Israel exile, and tragedy.

According to the word of the Lord, Ahijah the prophet stated:
About how Jeroboam would reap the fruit of his mistakes.
Beside the loss of five hundred thousand men in battle,
The death of Jeroboam was sudden- leaving all baffled.

Following the death of Jeroboam, Judah was elected as King,
However, this did not stop evil in Israel, from happening.
From perverting persons in the land, and practising idolatry,
Judah perverted Israel, hence provoking the Lord to jealousy.

In the fifth year of King Rehoboam's reign,
Israel's abominations of the Lord remained.
Then Shishak the King of Egypt was permitted by the Lord,
To go against Jerusalem in one accord.

King Shishak brought an allied army of nations against Judah alone.
And then fortified cities on his way to Jerusalem- taking the throne.
Following this, King Shishak took away treasures of all kinds,
From the house of the Lord and the Israel kingdom - inside.

On top of taking King Solomon's great wealth, he decided to also steal,
A total of 500 shields, made of bronze, gold, and steel.
Thus, King Rehoboam made bronze shields in their place:
And committed captains to guard them all- in haste.

Now the rest of the acts of Rehoboam were evil as time went.
And all because he replaced God, for a devilish torment.
Indeed, the two brothers- Rehoboam and Jeroboam were not alike,
Yet, the brothers both ended terribly- with no purpose of life.

The Reign of Abijam (Ref: 1 Kings, Chapter 15)

Abijah changed his name to Abijam.
To signify that he was a false God.
So, Abijam became king over Judah, for three years alone.
For God refused to bless his corruption and earthly throne.
Much like the infamous brothers that surpassed,
Abijam did not care at all, for chasing God's heart.

God grew weary, but would never give up,
On preserving the dynasty of King David.
And this wasn't because of the character of the descendants,
But for the character of God, whose mercies are endless.

Following Abijam, came King Solomon's grandson.
His name was Asa, and he put the idols at ransom.
Indeed, Asa followed in the same heart of King David,
Banishing perverted persons from the land,
Including Maachah- his own grandmother.

Asa's reign was thorough as much as righteousness,
For even when his family was in the wrong,
He did not hinder to stop their evil vices.

Despite all the good, Asa could not remove the high places,
Yet, successfully ensured that no idols were dedicated.
Nevertheless, Asa's heart was loyal to the Lord always,
From his power struggles with Baasha the King of Israel,
To the treasuries to buy favour of Ben-Hadad of Syria.

All the rest of the righteous acts of Asa,
Are they not written in this book?
He encouraged national piety,
And observation of solely God's law.

Alas, when Asa reached old age, his feet were diseased,
Due to his refusal to follow God's warning from Hanani.
Following Asa's death, Nadab took the kingship.
And sadly, did worse than his evil forefathers did.

Finally, God executed justice of Jeroboam's sin,
And had King Nadab to be assassinated- on a whim.

As Judah now had no king, Baasha, came through,
Despite not being a genetic descendant of Jeroboam,
God allowed this irony to take place,
Of another evil, rotten king to take over- after Jeroboam's place.

Baasha and The Ten Tribes (Ref: 1 Kings, Chapter 16)

God lifted Baasha out of the dust,
Making him ruler over the people of Israel.
This was a testament that God was behind the scenes,
Of Basha's involvement in assassinating Nadab- what a conspiracy!

As Baasha was a wicked King- no doubt,
God exuded His justice in Jeroboam's house.
So, although Baasha was not a blood descendant of Jeroboam,
He was a spiritual descendent of this great idolater,
And faced the same judgement- through and through.

From the North vs South,
Kingdoms continuing to be in dispute.
To Baasha's horrendous death,
Following with stray dogs that ate his corpse too.

It was considered a special disgrace for a King's dead corpse,
To be left out, wide in the open
And eaten by stray dogs.
Alas, Baasha did not have a proper burial for what he did,
And rested with his evil forefathers, before Elah was summoned.

Elah was the son of Baasha and provoked God the same.
Committed evil works, evil plots- using God's name in vain.
The word of the LORD came by the prophet Jehu: son of Hanani
And much like his good father, he said the hard truths.

The Bible tells us that by nature, God is merciful and gracious
Slow to anger and abounding in mercy and kind.
So, it took a lot of wickedness from Baasha and Elah,
To provoke anger in the might of the Lord.

Elah reigned two years in Tirzah with his servant Zimri.
Zimri helped Elah command half his chariots- before conspiring against him.
Indeed, by the twenty-seventh year of Asa's reign, Zimri attacked.
Fulfilling the prophecies that Baasha's household would be terminated,
And the Israelite dynasty of fifty years, would come to an end.

Zimri, the man who assassinated Elah,
Was rejected by the people at first glance.
So, Zimri took the rejection personally,
And reigned as king for a mere seven days.

With a dire end of Zimri's kingship- from suicide,
Omri was summoned as king over the Israelites.

As Omri had been the commander of the Israelite army,
Having him as king, made Israel live in harmony.
Indeed, Omri's democratic influence in Israel was great.
Making the Israelites feel content and safe.

Nevertheless, the harmony could only last for some time,
Before the people of Israel began to divide.
This time, the division was among their own tribes,
And half of the Israelites went to join anarchist- Tibni
Leaving half loyally back at Omri's side.

Omri built new buildings on the hills,
And opened new brimming cities too.
For instance, he opened the city of Samaria,
With excavations that withheld several sieges through.

The civil war, that led to Omri's eventual ruin and death,
Was another example of the Israelites' incorrigibleness,
A people divided against one another,
A nation who refused God- to win their repentance.

During the consecutive 41 years of King Asa's reign,
There was a total of 7 Israel kings.
All of which committed evil atrocities,
Hence blaspheming God's Holy Name.

Ahab, the son of Omri, marked as the eighth king to reign,
Distinguished another evil state.

From taking foreign wives by the number,
Thinking himself great enough to rebuild Jericho.
To committing idolatry,
Using virgins and corrupting widows,

Alas, Ahab proved to be a curse,
For all of Israel,
And according to the word of the LORD,
He was paving his path to hell.

Elijah, A Fiery Heart (Ref: 1 Kings, Chapter 17)

The name Elijah, means Yahweh is my God,
And rightly so, for this Tishbite,
Loved and followed the Lord.

Elijah was a fiery prophet- one of a kind,
He became a dominant spiritual force,
For Israel and its' people in due time.

Being part of the crucial time in history,
Elijah added a curse on Ahab- the wicked king.

Elijah famously proclaimed the following curse,
Be sure to read and ponder every word:

"As the LORD God of Israel lives
Before whom I, Elijah stand,
There shall no dew nor rain
On this grand land.

"Thus, only by my plea to the Lord,
Will you and your people,
Taste and see dew or rain again,
On the lands of this wicked world".

During the dark days of Ahab's apostasy,
Elijah's curse followed through.
And for three years straight,
There was no rain or even dew.

This was a dramatic demonstration against the pagan god- Baal,
Who was thought to control the weather as well.
Therefore, Elijah showed that a righteous man's prayers, do prevail,
And that God is mightier than any idol like Baal.

"As the Lord God of Israel lives, before whom I stand",
Was a statement that highlighted Elijah's nature and light,
Indeed, God was Elijah's source of strength and truth,
A door for the Israelites to stop their lawless deeds in sight.

The word of the Lord came to Elijah for another time.
He directed him eastward by the Brook of Cherith- to hide.
The Brook of Cherith, flew into the Jordan,
Providing Elijah with food from ravens, and clean water.

So, Elijah went and did according to the Lord's Word,
He went and stayed by the Brook of Cherith for safety,
Until God assured Elijah that he free from Ahab's threat.
And thereby could go back to prophesy again.

After being fed bread and meat by ravens,
To drinking water from the Brook of Cherith,
Elijah took forth- following the spirit of the law,
Prepared to face off King Ahab, once for all.

With no rain or dew in the land for three consecutive years,
It was no surprise that King Ahab seemed displeased.
He was displeased to see Elijah, let alone hear about his advice,
Therefore, he was adamant to rely on God this time.

With little budging with King Ahab, here and there,
The Lord showed mercy to the kingdom of Israel.
Rain and dew poured through to save livestock and harvest,
A little reprieve from the famine that started.

Then the word of the LORD came to Elijah again:
"Arise, go to Zarephath, with no hesitation".

So, Elijah once again followed through the Lord's command.
And when he came to the gate of that city- Zarephath,
He was happily received,
By a son and widow who needed a reprieve.

The Gentile widow was kind, but clearly struggling to make ends meet,
So, Elijah's presence in her house, was very neat.
It was as if God's chance for her and her son to go on,
It was a sweet gift from God's hand, all along.

And when that Gentile widow was out there gathering sticks,
Elijah requested her to bring water in a cup to drink.

With full faith and the little she had left,
She poured the water and brought him a morsel of bread.

Indeed, out of her generosity to give all she had,
God allowed Elijah to make her household glad.
So, through faith in God's power to abundantly provide,
Elijah the prophet stated, "Do not fear", as a reminder.

"Go and do as you have said,
But make me a small cake first"
At those words, the widow made this food,
A small gesture that blessed her abundantly too.

Indeed, as the widow humbly obeyed,
Her jar of oil and bin of flour never went away.
Much like Elijah's prayer for the Lord to not send rain or dew,
His prayer for the widow and son's eternal providence, came through.

Now it happened a few weeks later,
That the widow's son fell terribly sick.
This stress made the widow heartbroken,
And confused to even think.

Initially, the widow thought if she was wrong,
And if Elijah was really a man of God.
Her questions and doubts came sprawling,
Leading her to fall to the ground, tears brawling.

Elijah, being a prophet from birth- not choice.
Knew that he had to embrace the son and make some noise.
So, he called on God aloud, to show His mercy again,
And make this widow's son, an alive young man.

Glory to God alone, for this second miracle had occurred.
Making the widow and her son, feel loved and heard.

Samaria's Famine (Ref: 1 Kings, Chapter 18)

And it came to pass *after* many days,
That the word of the LORD finally came.
To Elijah, in the third year, that is
Saying, "Go, present yourself,
To Ahab, the wicked king,
And man made for Hell" .

So, Elijah obeyed with no hesitation,
Off to proudly present himself,
During the severe famine,
Occurring now all the way to Samaria.

Being three years now with this famine and drought,
King Ahab would be angry with Elijah- no doubt.
Now, as Obadiah oversaw King Ahab's house,
Elijah's presence made words of fear, roll from his mouth.

"Are you here to kill me, Elijah?
For I cannot say that you are here.
If King Ahab hears from me that you are here.
He will certainly scream and shout".

The prophet Elijah assured him that he would be safe,
After all, the Lord saw how he helped keep people safe.
From the one hundred prophets – fifty he sent to a cave.
Obadiah was certainly a man of integrity and loyalty of faith.

Elijah then kindly bid Obadiah final thanks and a farewell,
As he intended to meet King Ahab and his wicked wife-Jezebel.
Then it happened when Ahab saw Elijah,
That his whole demeanour became dire.

"Is that you, O troubler of Israel?
Must be nice to see me doing well?

Indeed, Ahab was easily the worst and ungodliest king,
With no reverence to God- he was demeaning.

Elijah then decided to challenge King Ahab,
And show him that God was the true one after all.
"Gather all Israel to me on Mount Carmel"
And may we see if we should worship God, or this Baal.

The special patron of Baal- Jezebel the queen,
Was intrigued and encouraged King Ahab to be mean.
So, King Ahab insulted Elijah before taking on his challenge,
And rounded his Baal worshippers to Mount Carmel.

All their cries to the weather 'god' Baal,
Were ineffective and not taken seriously at all.
"How long will you falter between two opinions?
If the LORD is God, follow Him".

This was a logical and useful question by Elijah the prophet,
For in general, the people of Israel were spiritually concocted.
But the people answered him not a word.
For they lacked courage to take back their word.

Then Elijah said to the people:
"I alone am left a prophet of the LORD.
But Baal's false prophets *are* four hundred and fifty.
Therefore, let them give us two bulls.
And let them choose one bull for their victory".

So, they took the bull which was given them
And they prepared it and called on the name of Baal.
From morning even till noon,
They were saying, "O Baal, hear us and come soon!"

But *there was* no voice.
Yes, no one answered at all.

So, the false prophets leaped,
In and about the altar.

And so it was, at noon,
That Elijah mocked them and said:
"Cry aloud, for he *is* a 'god';
Perhaps he is sleeping- are you sure he's not dead? "

At this mockery, the false prophets began to cry out,
And cut themselves, as was their custom, with lances and knives.
Until the blood gushed out on them by midday,
Their efforts were in vain and truly vile.

These false prophets had zeal,
As Elijah so humbly observed.
Yet, the zeal was without knowledge.
Therefore, their zeal profited them *nothing*.

Indeed, there was no voice from Baal,
Not one answer or payment of attention.
Then Elijah said to all the people:
"Come near to me".
And all the people came near to him.
Desperate to witness a divine intervention.

With this desperation made clear,
Elijah began to repair,
From the altar of the LORD
To the twelve stones that he could tether.
He placed the stones in a trench around the altar.

This symbolised the twelve sons of Jacob,
And how the Lord came and called Jacob "Israel".
Then, in the trench, he pulled wood in order,
Before cutting the pieces of bull meat.

Following this, he filled four waterpots to the brim.
And after doing these three consecutive times,
He went around the altar with confidence,
For he knew that water would not stop God igniting.

Without further ado, Elijah the prophet prayed:
"LORD God of Father Abraham, Isaac, and Israel,
Let it be known this day that You are God in Israel.
For I am Your servant, and have done all these things,
So, please hear me, that this people may know that You are the LORD".

After reciting this prayer, the showdown came through,
And God indeed sent fire to the sacrifice- fully consumed.
On top of this, the fire also licked up the water in trench,
Making this miracle unlike any other met.

So, when all the people saw it,
They fell on their faces.
And they said, "The LORD, He *is* God!
The LORD, He *is* God!" .

And Elijah said to them,
"Amen to that!
And now seize the false prophets of Baal!
Do not hesitate,
And may not one escape!".

Then Elijah said to Ahab,
"Go up, eat and drink.
For *there is* the sound of abundance of rain."
So, Ahab went up to eat and drink with disdain.

And Elijah went up to the top of Carmel.
Then he bowed down on the ground,
And put his face between his knees,
Before asking his servant, "To get up and look toward the sea"

Accordingly, the servant went up, looked, and said,
"There is nothing for all these seven times."
But at the seventh time where he went, he noticed a cloud.
It was a cloud as small as a man's hand.

And as he noticed this, he cried out,
"Elijah, there is a cloud, as small as a man's hand,
And it's rising out of the sea!"
So, Elijah said, "Go up, say to Ahab,
"Prepare *your chariot,*
*A*nd go down before the rain stops- you clown".

Now it happened in the meantime,
That the sky became black with clouds and wind.
And with the heavier rain,
Ahab rode away and went to Jezreel.

Then the hand of the LORD came upon Elijah.
And he girded up his loins,
And started running for fourteen miles.

This was obviously a supernatural power from God,
For Elijah to run for so long.
And we don't know exactly why he did this marathon.
Perhaps Elijah wanted to be first to infuriate Queen Jezebel- how fun!

God Encourages Elijah (Ref: 1 Kings, Chapter 19)

Ahab told Jezebel all that Elijah had done.
Also, how he had executed the prophets, one by one.
Then Jezebel sent a messenger to Elijah, saying,
"So let the gods do *to me,* and more also,
For if I do not make your life as the life of one of them by tomorrow".

With shattered confidence, Elijah arose,
And instead of running to infuriate her,

He turned to run for hills of Beersheba,
Leaving his servant to save his own life.

We cannot say for certain if this was led of God.
For God wanted to protect Elijah,
But we cannot say if God wanted to protect him at Jezreel,
Or protect him by getting him out of Jezreel.
Nevertheless, Elijah went about 80 miles south to Beersheba.

After a day's journey, Elijah found refuge under a broom tree.
And he prayed that he might die, and said,
"It is enough! Now, LORD, take my life
For I *am* no better than my fathers, I am in strife!"

Then as he lay and slept under a broom tree,
Suddenly an angel touched him, and said gently,
"Arise *and* eat."
Then he looked, and there by his head *was* a cake baked on coals,
Along with a jar of water- still cold.

Elijah ate and drank and lay down again.
And the angel of the LORD came back and touched him.
"Arise *and* eat, because the journey *is* too great for you."
So, Elijah rose again and ate and drank
Gaining much needed strength from the water and food.
From lack of sustenance to spiritual depression,
This was an act of God's mercy and compassion.

God allowed Elijah to release his frustrations,
And there he went into a cave to spend the night.
Then the word of the LORD came to him saying,
"What are you doing here, Elijah?
"Why are you not hearing?"

In response, Elijah assured his zeal for the Lord.
Yet, he felt alone and torn down,

From the killing of the Lord's prophets,
To the corruption he saw all around.

Indeed, discouraging times make God's servants feel more alone,
For this is exactly what Elijah felt in this moment of time.
Strangely, the reasons Elijah provided were crucial,
For if he was really the last prophet of God- as he thought,
He had to stay alive for this very purpose.

Then the Lord said, "Go out, and stand,
On the mountain before Me, the LORD."
And behold, the LORD passed by,
With a great and strong wind into the mountains by.

Into the mountains, the wind broke the rocks in pieces,
But the LORD *was* not in the wind.
And after the wind an earthquake occurred,
But the LORD *was* not in the earthquake- how absurd.

And after the earthquake, a fire came
But the LORD *was* not in the fire aflame.
So, the Lord finally revealed himself,
But not in loud commotion- rather in a still small voice.

The still small voice was exactly what the depressed Elijah needed,
A soft encounter with God, was a phenomenal experience.
So it was when Elijah heard *it,* that he used a mantle,
And wrapped his face, falling on it, and trembled.

"What are you doing here, Elijah?", God asked,
"Now go return your way at last".
This clearly showed how Elijah needed to get on,
And fulfil what God intended all along.

God had more work for Elijah to do.
He would also demonstrate God's choice of a king- **Jehu.**

Then, he would go visit a man - named Elisha,
And later befriend him, as much as be his "prophet teacher".

This both assured Elijah that he was not without help,
And that his work as a prophet was felt.

Therefore, he departed from there,
And found Elisha the son of Shaphat- as God said.
Elisha at the time, was with twelve oxen, plowing.
Then Elijah passed by him and threw his mantle,
To signal Elisha to quickly follow him.

Then Elisha left the oxen, ran after Elijah, and said,
"Please let me kiss my father and my mother again".
Elijah said to him, "Go back again, for what have I done to you?"

Thus, Elisha turned back briefly from him, and took this very chance,
To quickly threw a going- away party, for his family and friends.

Destroy The Enemy (Ref: 1 Kings, Chapter 20)

Now Ben-Hadad the king of Syria,
Gathered all his forces together
Thirty-two kings were with him.
With horses and chariots to win.

Ben-Hadad then besieged Samaria,
Making a civil war against it.
Then messengers were sent into the city,
To deliver a message to Ahab the king.

These messengers of Israel then said:
"Thus, your silver and your gold are Beh Hadad's now.
And your loveliest wives and children- what now?"

With this King Ahab replied with fear,
"My lord, O king, just as you say,

I and all that I have are yours too".
Then the messengers came back and said,
"Thus, it shall be, and that whatever is pleasant in your eyes,
You will give to Ben Hadad- with no compromise".

King Ahab called all the elders of the land and said,
"Notice, please, and see how this *man* seeks trouble,
For he sent to me for my wives, children, silver, and gold.
And I did not deny him- not once at all",

Yet, all the elders and all the people said to him,
"Do not consent to do this- why even listen to this threat?".
With this advice, King Ahab said to the messengers of Ben-Hadad,
"Tell my lord the king, 'That the sovereignty he wants, will not do".

And the messengers departed and told Ben-Hadad this news,
Then Ben-Hadad sent to him and said,
"The gods do so to me, and more also,
If enough dust is left of Samaria, we shall not falter".

"Get ready", King Ahab cried out,
And he and his army, went to attack.
Though it was uncharacteristically bold speech,
It was also a wonderful wisdom piece.

Thus, Syria and its allies readied themselves back,
And the city of Samaria braced for a furious attack.
Suddenly a prophet approached Ahab king of Israel, to say,
"Thus says the LORD: 'Have you seen all this great multitude?
Behold, I will deliver it into your hand today
And you shall know that I *am* the LORD who saves".

King Ahab was confused and asked, "By whom?"
And the prophet replied, "Thus says the LORD:
'By the young leaders of the provinces in the room".

Then King Ahab wondered, "Who will set the battle in place?"
And the prophet responded, "You, for this battle is in haste".
With that, King Ahab mustered the young leaders of the provinces,
Rounding up a total of two hundred and thirty-two.
To add, King Ahab guided the children of Israel- seven thousand,
To join the battle, and fight to the death- all around.

The battle went out all the way at noon.
Ben-Hadad and the kings helping him in total, were thirty-two.
Likewise, the young leaders of the provinces went out first.
And Ben-Hadad sent out a drunken patrol.

"Men are coming out of Samaria!"
With this announcement, Ben-Hadad said,
"If they have come out for peace, take them alive.
And if they have come out for war, take them alive instead".

Then these young leaders of the provinces went out with the army,
Each one killed his man; so, the Syrians fled while Israel pursued them.
King Ahab went out and attacked the horses and chariots,
Killing the Syrians with a great slaughter.
Indeed, this plan was more successful than,
King Ahab dared to imagine.

The prophet came to the king of Israel,
With a divine preparation at hand,
Then said to him, "Go, strengthen yourself.
Take note, and see what you should do in this land.
For in the spring of the year,
The king of Syria will come up against you".

Then the servants of the king of Syria said to him,
"Their gods *are* gods of the hills.
Therefore, they were stronger than we.
But if we fight against them in the plain, surely stronger we'll be.

Just dismiss the kings, each from his position,
And put captains in their places again.
Moreover, muster an army like the army lost,
Chariot for chariot and horse for horse.
Let us try again one more time,
And fight against them in the plain line".
With the fire inside the King of Syria,
He foolishly listened to his servants' large words.

Then the King of Syria's servants said to him again,
"Look now, we have heard Israel kings are merciful men.
Please, let us put sackcloth around our waists and ropes,
Around our heads and go out with heavy hope".

Indeed, they wore sackcloth around their waists,
And put ropes around their heads just the same.
To the king of Israel, they then said, "Your servant Ben-Hadad,
Implores your mercies to not take off his head".

Now the men were watching closely,
To see any sign of mercy,
The servants quickly grasped and said, "Your brother Ben-Hadad.
And this time the word brother touched King Ahab's head.

After, King Ahab said, "Go, bring him now with no rope".
So, Ben-Hadad came out to him.
Confirming that the cities that his father took, would be restored,
Ensuring King Ahab to set marketplaces in Damascus- in one accord.

King Ahab was pleased with this peaceful greeting,
Then created an official letter- a sort of treaty.

Now a certain man of the sons of the prophets said,
By the word of the LORD, "Strike me, please on my head".
And the man refused to strike him.
Then the prophet replied,

"Because you have not obeyed, you shall die".
Indeed, a lion found this man and killed him right away,
Proving the power God, to obey.

Now as the king passed by,
He cried out for one last time,
"Your servant went out into the midst of the battle.
And there, a man came over and brought now.
Be sure to guard this man.
And if by any means he is missing,
Your life shall be for his life,
Or else you shall pay a talent of silver for misleading".
Then the king of Israel assured him and replied,
"So shall your judgment be.
You yourself will truly decide".

The unknown prophet hastened to take,
The bandage away from his eyes at stake,
But as he began to do this compromise to his disguise from King Ahab,
Alas, he was recognized and killed in no time.

"Thus says the LORD: 'Because you have let slip whom I appointed,
Your life shall go for his life through,
And your people for his people too".
And with these words, King Ahab went to his house displeased,
Before travelling to Samaria for a light reprieve.

God's Justice (Ref: 1 Kings, Chapter 21)

And it came to pass after these things happened,
That Naboth the Jezreelite had a vineyard to tend
The vineyard was next to the palace of King Ahab,
Making him think that he could buy it from him.

"Give me your vineyard, that I may have it now,
For I want to make a vegetable garden, near my house,

And I will give you a vineyard better for it.
Or, if it seems good to you, I will give you its' money worth".

But Naboth said to King Ahab, "The LORD forbid,
That the inheritance of my forefathers, come to you, oh King!"
With that failure to negotiate,
King Ahab went sullen because of the word,
Which Naboth the Jezreelite had spoken.
And he lay down on his bed and turned away his face,
Refusing to eat food or talk with his wife in place.

But Jezebel his wife, came and pressed on him to talk,
"Why is your spirit so sullen that you eat no food at all?",
In response, King Ahab said, "Because I spoke to Naboth the Jezreelite,
And asked for his vineyard for a great money's worth.
Yet, he vehemently refused all my briberies".

Then Jezebel his wife, after listening to him vent,
Directed him to exercise authority over Israel including him!
"Arise, eat food, and let your heart be cheerful my king.
I will give you the vineyard of Naboth the Jezreelite".

Off the regal queen went,
Writing letters in King Ahab's name,
Sealing *them* with his seal,
And sending them to Naboth's way.

The nobles who *were* dwelling in the city with Naboth.
Were also coerced to join her mission.
"Proclaim a fast, and seat Naboth with high honour,
Then seat two men, scoundrels,
Who will falsely bear witness against him".

The nobles agreed to devise this evil plot,
Alas, Naboth was falsely accused of blasphemy,
Of the King Ahab and God,

Before taken forcibly out.

Naboth was then wrongly sentenced to die,
Thereby died because of being stoned by people nearby.
Then the nobles sent to Jezebel, saying with intent,
"Naboth has been stoned and is now dead".

So it was, when King Ahab heard that Naboth was dead,
That he got up and went down to take the vineyard- possession.

Then the word of the LORD came to Elijah the Tishbite,
"Arise, go down to meet Ahab king of Israel for this time.
In Samaria, he is at the vineyard of Naboth
An innocent man wrongly stoned to the death,
So go now,
Stop King Ahab,
He cannot take Naboth's vineyard for possession".

Thus said the LORD through Elijah again,
"Have you murdered the innocent,
And taken his precious possession?"
Know now that where dogs licked Naboth's blood,
The dogs shall lick your blood soon too.
For you provoke me to anger,
And you have led Israel along this path too.

With pointedly charges of two crimes,
King Ahab felt vexed for another time.
For Elijah's words of the Lord, spoke truth,
But he could not admit this to himself,
And certainly not his wife too.

Inspired by his messed-up notion of life,
And Jezebel- his regal and controlling wife,
King Ahab, sold himself to do wickedness,
Idol worship and corruption,

In the sight of the Lord.

So it was, when Ahab heard those words,
That he tore his clothes and put on a sackcloth,
To then fast all day,
And go into a deeply uncomfortable mourning.

And the word of the LORD came to Elijah the Tishbite,
"See how Ahab has humbled himself?
I will hear his cry.
So, I will not bring the calamity in his days.
But in the days of his son,
The calamity I planned, will come to play.

This act of mercy and compassion,
Proved again how God's prophecy of judgement,
Was never a threat against King Ahab's kingship,
But a wonderful door of mercy – an invitation.

Master of Disguise (Ref: 1 Kings, Chapter 22)

Now three years passed without war or hate,
Keeping peace between Syria and Israel in place.
Then it came to pass, in the third year,
That Jehoshaphat the king of Judah went down to fear.

This visit made the servants of Israel fear and ask the Israel King,
"Do you know that Ramoth in Gilead *is* ours?
For we hesitate to take it out of the Syrian king".

In response, the servants then went to Jehoshaphat to say,
"Will you go with me to fight at Ramoth Gilead today?"
Jehoshaphat added- instead of the servants so feeble,
"I *am* as you *are,* my horses as your horses,
And my people, are your people".

Jehoshaphat proposed then to seek God in the matter.
And with this bold request, King Ahab could not resist.
It wasn't surprising that King Ahab picked prophets,
For he hoped they would tell,
Words that he wanted to hear,
Hence saving him from the hand of King Jehoshaphat.

Hence, the king of Israel and Jehoshaphat the king of Judah,
Having both put on *their* robes,
Sat each on his luxurious throne.
Being at a threshing floor at the entrance of the Samarian gate,
They guided all 400 prophets, to prophesy before them- until late.

Zedekiah the son of Chenaanah, made horns of iron and said,
"With these you shall gore the Syrians until they are destroyed.'"
And then all the 400 prophets prophesied so, saying,
"Go up to Ramoth Gilead and prosper, for the LORD is at hand".

Then the messenger who had gone to call Micaiah spoke to him,
"Now listen, the words of the prophets with one accord,
Be sure to only encourage the king.
Please, let your word be like the word of one of them,
And speak encouragement only".

Hence, Micaiah said, "*As* the LORD lives, whatever the LORD says to me,
That I will speak, you shall see".
Then he came to the king; and the king said to him,
"Micaiah, shall we go to war against Ramoth Gilead?
And he answered him, "Go and prosper, for the LORD will deliver!"
Yet, when the king heard this, he was displeased.

"How many times shall I make you swear,
That you tell me nothing but the truth,
Not things I just want to hear?"

Indeed, the prophet Micaiah, was like Elijah- integrity through.
And said words of truth that shook King Ahab to the core.
Ahab hated him now because of the message he had said.
Clearly, his real conflict was with God,
But hatred against the prophet Micaiah, came out instead.

Then Micaiah calmly replied,
"I saw all Israel scattered on the mountains,
As sheep that have no shepherd- ready to die.
These have no master.
Let each return to his house in peace.
I am sorry if my words of the Lord,
Are making you feel displeased".

And the king of Israel said to Jehoshaphat,
"Did I not tell you he would not prophesy good concerning me, but evil?"
Indeed, King Ahab didn't consider that though Micaiah prophesied evil,
He unlike the 400 prophets before, prophesied the hard truth.

Then *Micaiah* said, "Therefore hear the word of the LORD:
I saw the LORD sitting on His throne,
And all the host of heaven standing in one accord.
On His right hand and on His left.
And the LORD then said,
'Who will persuade Ahab to go up,
That he may fall at Ramoth Gilead?'
So one spoke in this manner,
And another spoke in that manner.
Then a spirit came forward,
And stood before the LORD and said,
'I will persuade him.'

The LORD said to him,
'In what way?'

So, he said, 'I will go out and be a lying spirit,
In the mouth of all his prophets today.'
And the LORD said, 'You shall persuade *him,*
And prevail.
Go out and do so.
Do not delay'.

"Therefore look! The LORD has put a lying spirit in the mouth,
Of all these prophets of yours,
And the LORD has declared disaster against you,
From all accords".

Now Zedekiah the son of Chenaanah,
Went near and struck Micaiah on the cheek,
"Which way did the spirit from the LORD,
Go from me to speak to you- you pleb?"

Thus, Micaiah said, "Indeed, you shall see that on that day,
When you go into an inner chamber to hide.
That my prophesy was right.
And you will regret not heeding to it in time".

Hence, King Ahab now had words to say, "Take Micaiah,
And return him to Amon the governor instead.
For this governor shall put him in prison,
And give him water and some bread,

Following this turn of events,
Jehoshaphat and Ahab went into battle head.
At Ramoth Gilead, Ahab went off to disguise himself,
With hope that this would protect him from Micaiah's prophecy of death.

Now the king of Syria- Jehoshaphat, was saved in battle.
Leaving King Ahab killed, as Micaiah's had prophesied before.

When King Ahab's death became known, the battle was over.
And his body was brought to Samaria- the news was all over.
Then *someone* washed the chariot at a pool in Samaria,
And the dogs licked up his blood,
While the harlots bathed in it.

Fulfilling the word of the LORD which He had spoken.
Now the rest of the acts of King Ahab,
And all that he did,
The ivory house and cities which he built,
To all the sins that he dared to commit.
Are they not written in the book of the chronicles of the kings?
For King Ahab rested with his fathers,
Before his soon Ahaziah became rightful king.

It was the seventeenth year of Jehoshaphat king of Judah,
When Ahaziah became king over Israel.
He reigned for only two years,
But still committed a lot of evil.

For he served Baal and worshiped him,
Which again provoked the LORD God of Israel to anger,
Moreover, according to all that his father had committed.
Ahaziah was a king with no love for God, or moral conviction.

Ahaziah and Elijah
(Ref: 2 Kings, Chapter 1)

Moab rebelled against Israel after King Ahab's death.
Following that, King Ahaziah fell through the lattice,

The lattice was from his upper room in the Samaria land.
So, he was severely injured; and sent messengers to ask around,
Whether Baal-Zebub, the god of Ekron,
Would allow him to recover safe and sound.
Such a choice, showed that that Ahaziah was a true pagan,
For he turned to a Philistine idol- not God,
In his time of trouble and pain.

But the angel of the LORD said to Elijah the Tishbite,
"Arise, go up to meet the messengers of King Ahaziah,
Then inform him that he shall surely die.

Elijah departed with this prophetic announcement,
And informed the messengers of this fate.
Then King Ahaziah said to the messengers,
"What kind of man was it who told you so?"
So, they answered him, "A hairy man,

Who was wearing a leather belt around his waist as well".
And King Ahaziah knew of this description so right,
That this man was the prophet Elijah- the Tishbite.

Then the king sent to him a captain of fifty men,
He then went up to him.
Elijah was sitting on the top of a hill.
And heard the captain's orders to come down,

So, Elijah answered and said "If I *am* a man of God,
Then let me send fire to come down".
Indeed, fire came down from heaven,
Consuming the captain and the fifty men.
Yet, King Ahaziah would never give in.

Rather, King Ahaziah sent out another captain,
With fifty men under his command too,
All of whom asked Elijah the same task to do.
Like before, Elijah answered and said "If I *am* a man of God,
Then let me send fire to come down".
Indeed, fire came down once again.

Following this triumph in a row,
The angel of the LORD said to Elijah to go.
Elijah obeyed and went down to King Ahaziah- unafraid,
He was sure and prepared to beat his emotional shade.

Certainly, *Ahaziah* died according to the LORD's word,
Which Elijah had spoken, but no one heard.
And as Ahaziah had no son to take his place,
Jehoram became king in full haste.

By the second year of Jehoram's reign,
The son of Jehoshaphat, king of Judah was in disdain.
Now the rest of the acts of Ahaziah,
Are they not written,

In the book of the Chronicles,
And the wicked Kings of Israel?

Two Spirit Scoops (Ref: 2 Kings, Chapter 2)

Now it came to pass,
When the LORD was about,
That Elijah would leave the Earth,
By a cool whirlwind around.

Thus, Elijah took Elisha from Gilgal saying,
"Stay here, please, for the LORD is coming",
But Elisha said, "*As* the LORD lives,
And *as* your soul lives too,
I will not, ever, leave you!"

With no negotiation to tell,
Elijah and Elisha went to Bethel.
Now the sons of the prophets,
Who *were* at Bethel at that time,
Came out to Elisha saying, "It's time".

Time for what?" Elisha asked- all confused.
"Time for the Lord to take away,
Elijah, your master,
By a whirlwind, as you do".

Elijah asserted, "Yes, I know; keep silent!".
Making Elisha feel somewhat frightened.
Then Elijah said to him, "Elisha, stay here, please,
For the LORD has sent me".
But Elisha said, "*As* the LORD lives,
And *as* your soul lives too,
I will not, ever, leave you!"

With no negotiation to go,
Elijah and Elisha went to Jericho.

Now the sons of the prophets,
Who were at Jericho at that time,
Came running out to Elisha and said this time,
"Do you know that the LORD will take away,
Your master, Elijah by a whirlwind, today?"

Elisha again answered, "Yes, I know!".
Then Elijah said to him, "Stay here, please,
For the LORD has sent me on to the Jordan."
But Elisha said for the third time, "As the LORD lives,
And as your soul lives too,
I will not, ever, leave you!"

And off Elisha went by Elijah's side,
Along with fifty men,
Sons of the prophets at the time.
As all stood facing by the Jordan,
All stood contently from a distance.

Then, Elijah took his mantle, rolled it up tight,
Before striking water- making it divide.
So, Elijah and Elisha crossed over the Jordan River.
In a similar way as Moses had with the Red Sea.

With no time to spare, Elijah said to Elisha, "Ask! What you dare.
For I will do for you, anything.
Yes, whatever you need, say it true.
Before I am taken away from you".

So, Elisha said, "Please let a double portion of your spirit be.
A light in the dark, guiding me graciously".
With that request, Elijah replied:
"My boy, you have asked a hard thing.
Nevertheless, if you see me taken from you,
Rest assured that your request, shall be realised".

Then it happened, as they continued to chat,
That suddenly a chariot of fire with horses of fire intact.
This chariot of fire and horses separated the two of them.
Thus, Elijah went up by a whirlwind finally- into Heaven.

At the glorious sight, Elisha cried out,
"My father, my father, where are thou?
Until he saw him no more,
Elisha took hold of his own clothes.
And from his tight grip, his clothes tore.
He also took up the mantle of Elijah,
For the mantle had fallen on him,
And Elisha took off,
Until he was back at the Jordan River.

Then they said to him the following,
"Look now, there are fifty strong men,
Who are with your servants too?
Hence, let them go and search for your master,
Lest perhaps the LORD's spirit has taken him,
On a mountaintop, valley, or hill".

Elisha responded in full peace,
"You shall not send anyone as you please".
But when they urged him till, he was ashamed,
Elisha gave in to their cries and said,
"Send them out as you wish,
For perhaps they will find him!".

Therefore, they sent out the fifty men,
Who all searched for three days- amounting to nothing.
Alas, as Elisha already knew the outcome,
He could not claim anything, until they were undone.
Indeed, when the fifty men came back,
They pleaded to Elisha to reveal Elijah's tracks.
But all Elisha could say,

Was that Elijah had left already,
And that they should stop the search- right away.

Then the men of the city succumbed and said,
"Forgive our stubborn and stiff-necked nature.
Yet, please notice, the situation of this city of ours.
For it is pleasant, as my lord sees it.
But the water is bad by the gallon,
And the ground remains barren".

Following this lengthy conversation,
Elisha said, "Bring me a new bowl with salt in it".
After completing what Elisha had requested,
The word of the Lord, spoke through Elisha again.
"As the Lord heals this water before you.
He will ensure no more death or barrenness comes too".
Indeed, the water remained healed as Elisha spoke through the Lord.
Leaving the fifty men gobsmacked and glorifying the Lord.

Following these events, Elisha went up to Bethel again.
As he was going up the road, forty-two youths mocked him.
"Go up, you baldhead!" they cried twice in rudeness and pride.
Thus, Elisha turned around, looked at them,
Pronounced a curse strikingly.
Resulting the forty-two youths to be mauled to death,
By two female bears swiftly.

Following the horrid death of rude youths in Bethel,
Elisha went from there to Mount Carmel.
Then, after his services at Mount Carmel, were realised,
Elisha returned to Samaria for a short time.

Blood In The Water (Ref: 2 Kings, Chapter 3)

Now Jehoram the son of Ahab,
As king over Israel at Samaria.

Reigned during the eighteenth year,
Of Jehoshaphat the infamous king of Judah.

Jehoram reigned for twelve years in one accord,
Doing evil just like his father.
In the sight of the LORD.

Although he had put away the sacred pillar of Baal,
He persisted in the sins of Jeroboam the son of Nebat.
Making the rest of the Israelite people to sin,
And not depart from them.

Now as Mesha king of Moab, was a sheep breeder by trade,
He gave a total of one hundred thousand lambs,
Along with one hundred thousand rams,
To King Ahab- the Israelite King.

When King Ahab died, that the king of Moab chose to rebel,
Thereby planned to attack the kingdom of Israel.
As the Moabites lived on the eastern side of the Dead Sea,
The King of Moab saw an escape from taxation, as an opportunity.

Thus, King Jehoram went out of Samaria at that time,
Mustering all of Israel, one at a time.
Then he went and sent to Jehoshaphat king of Judah, saying,
"The king of Moab has rebelled against me".

"Will you go with me to fight against Moab?", King Jehoram asked.
In response, King Jehoshaphat replied with ease:
I am as you are: my horses as your horses,
My men as your men; so, I'll go as you please".

Nevertheless, King Jehoram and King Jehoshaphat allied,
Going into the Wilderness of Edom by night.

Their armies marched on that roundabout route seven days.
There was no water for the army or the animals that stayed.

Thus, the king of Israel said with no fear:
"Alas! For the LORD has called these three kings here.
Therefore, the Lord will deliver them into Moab's hand – have no fear".

But Jehoshaphat said, "Is there no prophet of the LORD here to inquire?
So, one of the servants of the king of Israel gave in to conspire,
"Elisha the son of Shaphat is here, who poured water on the hands of Elijah",
At the servant's word, Jehoshaphat said, "The word of the LORD is with him."

Hence, both kings went down to him,
Then, Elisha said to the king of Israel,
"What have I to do with you?
Go to the prophets of your father,
And the prophets of your mother".

Clearly, as Elisha would not stand with the two kings,
He brought to them a musician in their presence.

Then it happened, when the musician played,
That the hand of the LORD came upon him to say:
"Thus says the LORD: 'Make this valley full of ditches.
For thus says the Lord: 'You shall not see wind.
Nor shall you see an ounce of rain.
Yet that valley shall be filled with water,
So that you, your cattle, and animals may drink the same".

This prophecy was a simple matter in the sight of the LORD.
Showcasing He'd deliver two kings to the Moabites, in one accord.
Every fortified city and every choice city were attacked.

Along with every good tree cut down to the ground.
To make matters worse, the spring of water came out,
To turn every good piece of land with stones laid out".

Now it happened in the morning after the grain offering was offered,
That suddenly water came by way of Edom- filling the land with water.
Thus, when all the Moabites heard this.
They were able to bear arms and the older were gathered.
All the Moabites rose early in the morning and set at the border.
Later seeing the colour red, as blood, filling up the whole water.

At this sight, they said in reverence and fear,
"This is blood; the kings have surely struck swords here.
This is a symbol of how they have killed one another with no mercy.
So, the Lord is due to punish us all accordingly.

When they came to the camp of Israel,
Israel rose and attacked the Moabites there.
As the Moabites fled before them.
The camp of Israel entered their land.

The Israel army killed the Moabites at ease.
Before looting and destroying all their cities.

Each man threw a stone on every good piece of land,
Stopped up all the springs of the water,
Along with cutting down the good trees by the border.
Only the stones of Kir Haraseth were left intact.
However, the slingers surrounded and had it attacked.

When the king of Moab saw that the battle was too ferocious,
He took with him seven hundred men who drew their swords.
They all then broke through to the king of Edom,
But their efforts failed through and through.

As a final try, the King of Moab, took his eldest son,
Who would have reigned in his place if they won.
Hence, he offered his son as a burnt offering upon the wall.
Creating a great indignation against Israel.

Operation, Dead Child (Ref: 2 Kings, Chapter 4)

"Your servant my husband is dead,
And you know that your servant's intents".
This woman's words were of clear pain.
For her loss- as a wife of the sons of the prophets, wasn't the same.

Hence, Elisha said to her, "What shall I do for you?
Yes, please tell me, what do you have in the house?"
In response to his compassion, the woman said,
"Your maidservant has nothing to offer or give,
Except of a mere jar of oil".

With that Elisha replied with joy,
"Alright, go, borrow vessels from everywhere.
Take empty vessels from all your neighbours that care.
Hence, she went from him and shut the door,
Before bringing a myriad of vessels for Elisha to pour.
And he said, "Go, sell the oil, and pay your debt.
For now, you and your sons, live on the rest."

Now it happened one day that Elisha went to Shunem,
That there came a very notable woman.
This woman persuaded him to eat some food.
So it was, as often as he passed by, he would eat.

"Look now, I know that this is a holy man of God,
For he passes by us regularly and with a heart of love.
Therefore, please, let us make a small upper room on the wall.
With a bed, a table, a lampstand, and chair.
So that whenever he comes to us, he can turn in there".

Indeed, the woman and her husband prepared this small upper room.
Sooner or later, Elisha with much persuasion, resided down there.
Then Elisha said to Gehazi his servant,
"Call this Shunammite woman at once".

When he had called her, she stood before him with purity.
Before stating "Please let me know what you have been concerning".
After much back and forth with Gehazi- who spoke on Elisha's behalf,
The woman was promised the gift of a healthy and happy son.

So it was, after a year's time- according to Elisha's prophecy.
That this woman conceived a son
Who grew up healthy and happy.

Now it happened one day,
That the son went out to his father- who was reaping crops.
Crying out saying: "My head, my head, it hurts!"

The servant helped the father to carry the boy,
All the way to their mother inside.
They were on their knees praying until noontime.
But despite their efforts, the boy- their son, died.

Then the mother called to her husband, and said,
"Please send me one of the donkeys and young men.
The husband replied with agony and pain,
"It is neither the New Moon nor the Sabbath.
So, tell me why you are going to him today?"
Nevertheless, she said to her husband with tears, "It is well,
Be sure to hold onto hope my dear",

With that she took off with a donkey and servant.
When the man of God- Elisha saw her afar off at Mount Carmel,
He said to his servant Gehazi, "Look, the Shunammite woman looks unwell!

Please run now to meet her, and check if she, her husband, and son, are okay".

"Did I ask a son for my family to love and nurture?
Did I not say to not deceive me further?"
With those words that cut deep, Elisha knew,
That her son had died, and he had to heal him too.

When they arrived at the house to see the bed,
Elisha found the boy, their son, still lying dead,
He went in therefore, shut the door behind the two of them,
Before praying to the Lord to bring life to the boy again.

After praying and laying his presence,
The child became warm all over the flesh.
With that, Elisha paced back and forth,
Until the child sneezed seven times,
And finally, by God's grace, opened his eyes.

Elisha then called Gehazi and said,
"Call this Shunammite woman and the child's dad".
So Gehazi called her and the husband inside.
Leading both hopeful parents to embrace their son.

Elisha returned to Gilgal- for there- the famine all over.
Hence, the sons of the prophets, caught his attention.
Elisha then ordered his servant to prepare.
A large pot, with boiled stew,
To feed the sons of the prophets there.

Now it happened, as they were eating the stew,
That they cried out and said, "Man of God, there is death", so they could not eat.
Thus, Elisha then said, "Bring some flour and serve to the people, all of it."

Then a man came from Baal Shalisha, brought the man of God,
Twenty loaves of barley bread,
And newly ripened grain instead.

Indeed, after he set this before them.
All the people ate and were filled.
And there was some food left over,
As the Lord had previously willed.

Naaman, The General (Ref: 2 Kings, Chapter 5)

Now Naaman, general of the Syrian king army,
Was a great and honourable man in the eyes of everybody.
Although a leper, he was a mighty man of valour.
Hence, the LORD helped him give victory to Syria.

After the Syrians had gone out on raids,
A young girl was held captive from the land of Israel.
The young girl waited on Naaman's wife.
Then she said to her mistress,
"If only my master were with the prophet in the Samaria city!
For if so, he would surely heal him of his leprosy".

Thus, Naaman went in and told his master, saying,
"Thus, and thus said the girl who is from the land of Israel".
Then the king of Syria said, "Go now, and I'll send a letter to the Israel King".
So Naaman departed with haste,
Taking ten talents of silver, six thousand shekels of gold,
Along with ten changes of clothing with him.

Once the letter was brought to the Israel King's eyes,
The King of Israel tore his clothes and began to patronize:
"Am I God, to kill and make alive or dead?
How could he think I could heal his leprosy then?

So it was, when Elisha the man of God heard this event,
That he asked to come and talk with him.
"Why have you torn your clothes?
Please let him come to me- an Israelite prophet,
So that the truth will be known.

Then Naaman went with his horses and chariot,
Standing at the door of the prophet Elisha's house.
And Elisha sent a messenger to him, saying,
"Go and wash in the Jordan seven times,
And your flesh shall be restored and clean".

But at those humbling words and tasks,
Naaman became furious in all parts.
For Namaan expected Elisha to wave his hand,
And to God, simply pray,
For his unflattering leprosy,
To finally go away.

"Are not the Abanah and the Pharpar,
The rivers of Damascus better than,
All the waters of Israel in the land?
To add, could I not wash in them from the start,
And be clean from this leprosy, you lark!"

With those harsh words, Namaan turned away in a rage.
And his servants-built courage to finally relay,
"My father, if the prophet had told you to do something great,
Would you not have done it right this way?"

Thanks to the servant's encouragement and patience,
Naaman succumbed to Elisha's initial instructions.
Indeed, Naaman went down and dipped seven times in the Jordan,
And as promised, his flesh became like a little child, all clean.

Following this miraculous course of events,
Naaman returned to the man of God again.
Along with all his aides, Naman urged Elisha to accept the gifts arrayed,
As a token of his gratitude for taking his ailing leprosy away.

Nevertheless, Elisha politely refused all the gifts,
Leaving Naaman to say this,
"Then, if not, please let your servant be given two mule-loads on the earth.
To no longer offer burnt offering or sacrifices from the dirt.
Also, please ask the Lord to pardon your servant:

For where my master goes into the temple of Rimmon,
I will have to play the part and bow down.
Then, Elisha replied with grace,
"Go in peace and keep the faith."

So Naaman departed from him a short distance away.
But Gehazi, the servant of Elisha pursued his fame.
So, Gehazi ran to Naaman, until he noticed,
And falsely asked him for gifts as a bonus.

Thus, Naaman gave Gehazi two talents of silver,
Along with two bags and changes of garments.
When he came to the citadel,
He took them from their hand,
And stored them away in the house.
Before the men departed.

Now Gehazi went in and stood before Elisha's way.
Before being asked: "Where did you go today ?"
Gehzai responded ever so readily,
"Oh, Elisha, I did not go anywhere really".

As Elisha knew this was a big lie,
He stated the following curse on the line:
As you turned back to Naamaan for gifts,
You shall have his leprosy.
And it shall cling to all your descendants.

As it was said, it occrued right away,
That Gehazi's skin turn white as snow,
With spots of leprosy bright as day.

Surrounded By God (Ref: 2 Kings, Chapter 6)

The sons of the prophets said to Elisha lightly,
"See now, the place where we dwell, fits too tightly".
Hence, Elisha allowed them to go to the Jordan,
To let every man, take a beam from there to dwell.

Elisha decided to go with them and give them help.
As they arrived at the Jordan, they cut down the trees.
Alas, the iron axe head fell in the water unceremoniously,
Making them anguished as they had borrowed it previously.

So, Elisha took a stick and cut it in half,
Before throwing it out in the water, making the iron float.
"Pick it up for yourself", he instructed the sons of the prophets to do.
And they did, reaching out and taking the iron axe head through.

At the time, the king of Syria was making war,
A war against Israel disheartening the people- like before.
The Syrian king consulted with his servants and planned.
To raid all of Israel, by setting up a hidden camp.

The king of Israel sent someone to the land of Dothan,
As it was where Elisha was residing in.
Thus, Elisha warned him of the Syrian king's plans of warfare,
Prompting the king of Israel to send horses, chariots, and the army at night,

Surrounding the city and keeping the Israelites people under their care.

"Alas, my master! What shall we do?",
As Elisha's new servant asked clearly scared.
Elisha answered, "Do not fear,
For those who are with us,
Are more than who are there".

Elisha then prayed to the Lord,
To open his servants' eyes to see.
Then the LORD opened the eyes of this humble servant,
And behold horses and chariots of fire were seen,
All around Elisha and across the mountains.

When the Syrians came down to him,
Elisha prayed to the LORD, and said,
"Strike this people, I pray, with blindness instead".

Therefore, the Lord, heeded to Elisha's word,
Striking the Syrian army with blindness.
"Follow me, for I'll bring you to the man you seek",
These words were deceptive of Elisha to speak.

Hence, Elisha led them to Samaria,
Before God opened their eyes again.
The Lord then instructed no killing to occur,
But for the King of Israel to offer them a great feast.

After they all ate and drank from the feast,
The Syrian raiders returned to their king.
And it happened after this that Ben-Hadad king of Syria,
Went up with his army to besiege Samaria.

Until a donkey's head was sold for eighty silver shekels,
Along with one-fourth of a kab of dove droppings for five silver shekels,

The Syrian raiders stopped raiding Samaria,
Giving some much-needed relief, to the people.

A woman cried out to the Israel King passing by,
"Help, my lord, O king, my son will be eaten alive!"
And he said, "If the LORD does not help you,
How can I?
But I advise you hide your son tonight.

So, the woman heeded to the Israel King
And hid her son from then next morning.

Elisha was sitting in his house with the elders,
But before the messenger came to him, he said,
"Do you see how this son of a murderer has sent,
A person to take away my head?
Be sure now to look, when the messenger comes,

Indeed, Elisha had the door shut tight,
In response the king of Israel cried,
"Surely this calamity is from the Lord above,
So, why should I wait any longer".

God's Miraculous Provision (Ref: 2 Kings, Chapter 7)

Then Elisha said, "Hear the word of the LORD.
As tomorrow about this time,
A seah of fine flour and two seahs of barley,
Shall be sold for a shekel on Samaria's gate line.

Following this, an officer on whose hand the king leaned,
Answered the man of God quickly,
"Look, if the LORD would make windows in heaven,
Could this thing be?"
In response, the man of God said,
"In fact, you shall see it with your eyes,
But of it, you shall not eat".

Now there were four leprous men,
Standing at the entrance of the gate.
All four leprous men said to one another,
"Why are we sitting here until we die from fate?

The four planned to enter the city,
As the famine in the city was great.
Hence, not even the Syrian army noticed their entry,
For they left their lives, up to fate.

At the outskirts of the Syrian camp,
The four men were wonderfully surprised.
For the Lord had caused the army of the Syrians,
To hear the noise of chariots and horses—hence going out.

"Look, the king of Israel has hired against us,
The Hittites' and Egyptians' Kings to attack!"
Therefore, the Syrian army fled at twilight,
Leaving their entire camp: tents, horses, and donkeys,
In attempt to preserving their own lives.

Hence, these four lepers became opportunists,
As they began to loot freely from the vacant Syrian camp.
From going in and out of one tent to eat and drink,
They begin to carry out silver, gold, and elegant clothing.

Then they said to one another,
"We are not doing right.
As this day is a day of good news,
And we remain silent until morning light,
A punishment will come upon us all.
Therefore, to the king's household, shall we now go".

Indeed, the four leprous men went out with ease.
Calling out to the gatekeepers of the city.

After explaining their situation in full truth.
The gatekeepers allowed them to enter through.

As the king of Israel arose in the night,
He asked the men to explain all things right.
So, the four leprous men heeded to the king's command,
Pleading with him to accept the foods they took from the Syrian camp.

All the road was full of garments and weapons,
Which the Syrians had thrown away in haste.
Thus, the under the King of Israel's green light to go,
The people of Israel went out and plundered the Syrian's tents.

Following the plundering and looting that happened 'til late,
The King of Israel appointed an officer to guard the gate.

Hence, as Elisha had prophesied the officer's terrible fate,
The very officer was trampled by the people,
Despite guarding them by the gate.

Elisha's Acts (Ref: 2 Kings, Chapter 8)

Then Elisha spoke to the woman- whose son he'd restored life.
Instructing her go out of her household for some time.
This was due to a famine that would come on her homeland,
A famine that would last for seven years at hand.

Thus, the woman arose and did according to what Elisha had said.
She took her household to dwell with the Philistines instead.
After the seven years had finally passed,
The woman and her household appealed to return at last.

Then the king talked with Gehazi,
Who was the former servant of Elisha.
Saying "tell me, please, all the great things,
For my mind on Elisha, has now wandered".

So, Gehazi said, "My lord, O king, this is the woman,
And this is her son,
Whom Elisha restored to life in front of everyone".
When the king heard this story alone, he accepted her return,
And appointed an officer to restore all that was hers.

Elisha then headed off to Damascus,
For Ben-Hadad- king of Syria was sick.
So, Elisha was asked to heal him,
Giving him hope from the disease.

Hazael went to meet Elisha and brought him a gift.
To plead with Elisha on recovering the Syrian King.
Elisha said to him, "Go, say to your king that he'll recover.
And after uttering this, Elisha began to cry.

At this sight, Hazael asked with concern,
"Why is my lord weeping now, are you hurt?"
Elisha answered that he knew that the strongholds set on fire,
Along with the young men to be killed with the sword.
To the children dashed and women ripped open,
Would make God filled with anger,
To take the King of Syria's life.

Thus, Hazael said, "But what is your servant—a dog,
To do or understand with this terrible and gross news?
And Elisha answered, "The LORD has shown me you".

With that Hazael understood that the king over Syria, would die.
And as a result, he would be appointed to be King overnight.
Indeed, Hazael's understanding and Elisha's prophecy came true,
For in the next day, after the thick cloth dipped with water, touched the king's face,
He died straight away, paying off his dues.

Reigning in the fifth year of King Joram.
Hazael did not choose war against Israel.

However, this did not make King Joram- thirty-two years old,
Any closer to God.

In fact, King Joram married his sister,
And did evil in the sight of the Lord and people.
Yet the LORD would not destroy Judah,
For the sake of his servant David- as promised.
However, God numbered King Joram's days,
As recorded in the book of Chronicles.

Fast forward, and Ahaziah the son of Jehoram, reigned over Judah.
Being a mere twenty-two years of age.
His mother's name was Athaliah,

Now, Ahaziah's mother was the granddaughter of Omri,
However, this did not make her wise or anything.
In fact, due to his mother playing with his head,
Ahaziah made war against the king of Syria at Ramoth Gilead.

Hence, after Zair and Libnah revolted at King Joram's time.
Ahaziah visited the now terribly sick, King Joram- as he was due to die.

The Annointing of Jehu (Ref: 2 Kings, Chapter 9)

Elisha called one of the sons of the prophets and said,
"Get yourself ready, take this flask of oil in your hand.
Then head out to Ramoth Gilead and look for Jehu,
Once you find him, take him to the inner room.

Indeed, the prophet heeded to what Elisha had said.
Leading Jehu the son of Jehoshaphat.
Once they entered the inner room, he took the flask of oil,
Poured it on Jehu's head, and said,
'Thus says the LORD: "I have anointed you king over Israel".

Jehu was then instructed to strike down the house of Ahab,
Avenging the blood that he shed savagely,
That of the Lord's servants and prophets.

Hence, the house of former king Ahab became like,
The house of Jeroboam the son of Nebat at the time.
Likewise, the dogs ate Jezebel on the plot of ground at Jezreel,
Leaving no place to bury her properly.

Then Jehu came out to the servants who then inquired,
"Is all well, my master, this time?
Thus, Jehu spoke freely- explaining,
How the Lord anointed him through the prophet,
To become the new Israelite king.

With this explanation like no other,
Each man hastened to take his garment,
And put it under.
As the garments were laid now on top of the steps.
Each man heeded to say, "Jehu is king!",
And they blowed the trumpets.

The first act of kingship that Jehu had conspired,
Was to attack King Joram,
As compensation for the previous wounds and harm,
Which the Syrian armies inflicted.

Hence, Jehu rode in a chariot and went to Jezreel,
For King Joram was laid up there by the field.
Now as Ahaziah king of Judah had come down to see,
There was a watchman who stood- on the tower in Jezreel.

After he saw the company of Jehu,
He then assigned a horseman too.
The horseman reported the events that were happening.
Confirming that there was war and treachery occurring.

Then Jehu said to Bidkar his captain
"Pick him up and throw him into the tract of the field".
Hence, the captain threw the body in the field of Naboth- the Jezreelite.

As Ahaziah king of Judah saw this scene, he fled.
Until he reached the area called the Gur Ascent.
After some rest, he fled to Megiddo with no moment to spare,
And before he knew it, he ended up dying there.

King Ahaziah's body was carried out by his loyal servants.
All of which carried him by a chariot to be buried in his tomb.
After the burial of King Ahaziah in Jerusalem with his fathers,
Jehu had come to Jezreel, and Jezebel heard of it.

Thus, Jezebel put paint on her eyes and adorned her head,
Whilst looking out through a window for a place to torment.
Hence, as Jehu entered at the gate, she said,
"Is it peace, Zimri, murderer of your master who fled?"

At those wicked words, Jehu looked up with a frown,
Before then appointing three eunuchs to throw her down.

With Jezebel's blood now spattered on the wall- all over,
Her body- being the king's daughter, was carried away.
However, as they were about to bury her into the ground,
Only her skull, feet, and the palms of her hands, were found.
Therefore, they came back and told King Jehu this.

King Jehu remembered what Elijah had prophesied long ago.
A prophesy that alluded that Jezebel would be eaten by dogs for show.
Indeed, this later occurred,
And the corpse of the wicked Jezebel,
Was eaten by the dogs, an unfortunate kind of burial.

Baal Falls (Ref: 2 Kings, Chapter 10)

As King Ahab had seventy sons in Samaria.
Jehu wrote and sent letters to Samaria saying:
"Now as soon as this letter comes to you now,
Since your master's sons are with, thou,

There are chariots and horses,
Along with weapons in the fortified city.
Thus, be sure to choose the best,
Only the qualified of your master's sons.
And set him on his father's throne,
To fight for your master's house".

At Jehu's written words, King Ahab's sons were exceedingly afraid.
For they knew that two kings couldn't stand up to him before.
So, they pondered what they could do,
As their chances of success, were few.

Hence, from those in charge of the city including the elders also,
Sent a letter to Jehu, saying, "We are your servants,
Thus, we will do all you tell us and want.
Also, we will not make anyone of us king.
Instead, we will do what you deem the right thing".

In response, Jehu wrote a second letter to them, saying:
"If you are for me and will obey my voice, I will show mercy.
But you must prove your loyalty to me.
So now, take the heads of the men,
And come to me at Jezreel,
By this time tomorrow, as one".

Now the king's sons, seventy persons as stated before,
Were with the great men of the city, ready to pour.
Alas, King Jehu tricked them for all to see,
Thereby ordering their heads to be cut off,
And placed in baskets sent to Jezreel.

Then a messenger came and told King Jehu, saying,
"They have brought the heads of the king's sons".
With those words, King Jehu said,
"Lay them in two heaps at gate entrance, until morning".

So it was, in the morning, that he went out and stood,
Proclaiming to all the people loudly,
"You are righteous, for indeed I conspired against,
Against my master that is,
And killed him with haste.

So, it was as the Lord spoke through his servant and prophet Elijah.
That the house of King Ahab, would perish in full time.

Following King Jehu's successful killing,
He ordered his great men to kill King Ahab's sons' close acquaintances,
Including the group of priests.
Only until no one from King Ahab's kingdom, remained.
King Jehu arose and departed for Samaria.

On the way, at Beth Eked of the Shepherds,
Jehu met with the brothers of Ahaziah -king of Judah, saying,
"Who are you?"
Hence, they answered,
"We are the brothers of Ahaziah.
We have come down to greet the sons of the king,
Along with the sons of the queen mother".
In reply, he cried.
"Take them alive!".
Thus, they took them alive,
And killed them at the well of Beth Eked too.
But the number of men killed this time,
Were merely forty-two.

Now when King Jehu departed from the place,
He met Jehonadab the son of Rechab with haste.
"Is your heart right, as my heart is toward your heart?"
And Jehonadab answered, "It is, trust me from the start".

King Jehu in reply, asserted with authority,
"If it is, give your strong hand to me".

Thus, he gave him his hand carefully,
Taking him into the chariot quickly.

Then King Jehu said, "Come with me,
To see my zeal for the LORD".

Hence, they had him ride in his chariot to Samaria.
Where he killed all who remained to Ahab,
Until all were destroyed,
Thereby fulfilling the word of the Lord.

Following this, he gathered all the people together to say:
"Ahab served Baal a little, Jehu will serve him all the way".
Therefore, they called the prophets of Baal- servants and priests,
To set up a magnificent sacrifice, ensuring no one missing would live.

Clearly, King Jehu acted deceptively, with the intent hidden,
Of destroying the worshipers of Baal, little by little.
Indeed, after all the worshippers of Baal, put their vestments,
King Jehu commanded Jehonadab the son of Rechab.
To go and search that no servants of the LORD were present.
So that he could order the captain to kill on his word,
All the worshipers of Baal, by the edge of the sword.

So, at King Jehu's word, the captain fulfilled the word,
Killing all the Baal worshippers with the edge of the sword.
Then the captain's helpers, brought the sacred pillars out,
From the temple to be burned throughout.
After the temple for Baal had finally come undone,
King Jehu ordered for it to stay as a refuse dump.

Thus, King Jehu destroyed Baal from Israel in a hot minute.
Alas, this good thing did not stop him from sinning too.
Therefore, the Lord began to cut off parts of Israel.
Enabling Hazael to conquer Israel's territories- large and small.

From the Jordan eastward:
To the land of Gilead— Gad, Reuben, and Manasseh
Along with Aroer, which is by the River Arnon,
Including Gilead and Bashan.
The lands of Israel were constantly being conquered.

This conquering trend continued for twenty-eight years,
Being the total time of King Jehu's reign.
Hence, only after burying King Jehu in Samaria -with his fathers-,
Did his son Jehoahaz reign as king,
And provide Israel with much needed allies and partners.

Killing Spree (Ref: 2 Kings, Chapter 11)

As Athaliah saw Ahaziah-her son, now dead,
She abruptly arose to destroy all royal heirs.
But when Jehosheba- daughter of King Joram and sister of Ahaziah heard,
She made sure Joash- the son of Ahaziah, would not be murdered.

Indeed, she stole Joash away from among the king's sons,
Hiding him with his nurse – in the house of the Lord.
Alas, even after Athaliah's murder rampage had stopped,
She forcibly reigned all over the land.
Causing Joash to remain hidden in the house of the Lord,
For a consecutive number of six years.

In the seventh year Jehoiada the priest, sent and brought,
Captains of hundreds— of the bodyguards and the escorts.
Likewise, Jehoiada brought the men into the house of the LORD,
To take an oath with the Lord- make a covenant.

As Joash was now revealed to Jehoiada's sight,
It was commanded that one third of the men on duty,
Would keep watch over the king's house on the Sabbath- at night,
Leaving one third of the men at the gate of Sur,
And another one third men at a gate behind the escorts.

Therefore, the valiant men kept watch over the Lord's house,
Preventing any break ins on the Sabbath.
From the contingents off duty, to the captains of hundreds,
Jehoida the priest, made sure all were armed.
Thus, spears and shields were used from King David's time,
From the altar, house, right side of the temple and the left side out.

After these events occurred, Jehoida brought out the king's son,
Placed a crown on him, showing him the Testimony.
Along with anointing his head, clapping their hands,
To calling out "Long live the king!" in front of everyone.

Now when Athaliah heard the noise,
From the escorts and the people,
Athaliah came out to the people.
Inside the Lord's temple.

There was the king standing by a pillar
Along with leaders and the trumpeters.
The sight was not rocketing science for Athaliah,
As she learned they were all rejoicing.

At that knowledge, she tore her clothes and cried,
"Treason! Treason you people burn my eyes!"
So, Jehoiada the priest commanded the captains of the hundred men,
To take her out of the house of the Lord and kill her somewhere.
Hence, the captains readily seized her; and took her outside.
Then, killed her by the sword, before everyone's eyes.

Jehoiada then made a covenant between,
The LORD, the king, and the people he pleased.
In addition, all the people of the land went.
To the temple of Baal and tore it down to the end.

After thoroughly breaking in pieces its' altars and images,
Jehoiada ordered Mattan the priest of Baal, to be killed.

Following the final blows against Baal's temple and priest,
The people of the land Israel finally lived in peace.
Indeed, the city was quiet, for they had slain Athaliah with the sword,
Thereby prompting them to assign Jehoash king.
Despite him being only seven years old.

The Reign Of King Jehoash (Ref: 2 Kings, Chapter 12)

In the seventh year of King Jehu's reign,
Jehoash became king in Jerusalem.
For a total of forty years, did Jehoash rule,
As he kept the Lord in the centre of everything.

Despite of Jehoash doing what was right in the sight of the Lord,
He did not take the high places away as the priest instructed him.
As a result, people still made sacrifices and incense,
To the false gods at those high places.

Jehoash then requested of the priests,
To take all the money of the dedicated gifts,
Along with the census money given from each one,
To be brought into the house of the LORD.
Therefore, using the gifts and every man's constituency,
The damages of the temple were due to be repaired.

Alas, by the twenty-third year of King Jehoash,
The priests failed to use the gifts or money to repair the temple's damages.
Grieving King Jehoash enough to call Jehoiada the priest,
Along with the other priests, in one accord.

"Why have you not repaired the damages of the temple?"
In response to King Jehoash's inquire,
The priests agreed to not receive more money,
From the king or the people.

After this, Jehoiada the priest took a chest,
Bored a hole in its lid, and on the altar, set.
As he did this, the other priests kept the door.
Allowing Jehoiada enough time to deliver the money,
From the chest to those who had been apportioned,
To oversee and fix the house of the Lord.

Hence, carpenters and builders,
To masons and stonecutters,
Along with people who bought timber,
Marbles and some hewn stone,
Were paid the money to repair the temple,
And take it back to its' prime.

Moreover, as the workmen dealt faithfully.
The money from the trespass offerings,
On top of the money from the sin offerings,
Weren't brought into the house of the Lord,
But instead, given to the priests to keep.

Now the rest of the acts of Joash,
And all that he did,
Are they not written,
In the book of the Chronicles?

From the chronicles on the kings of Judah,
Along with the servants who formed a conspiracy,
Thereby killing Joash in the house of the Millo,
A house that went through Silla.

Clearly, for Jozachar the son of Shimeath,
And Jehozabad the son of Shomer,
Joash's servants struck him to the death.
To bury him in City of David.

Allowing Amaziah his son,
To finally reign in his place.

Oppression Of Israel (Ref: 2 Kings, Chapter 13)

In the twenty-third year of Joash's reign,
The king Jehu completed his seventeen years.
Doing evil in the sight of the Lord,
Following all the sins of Jeroboam- his late father.

Thus, the anger of the LORD was aroused again,
Leading up the Israel being delivered into Hazael's hands again.
Following this deliverance to the King of Syria's rule,
Israel began to be oppressed and treated like a mule.

Then the LORD gave Israel a deliverer to escape,
From under the hand of the Syrians and children of Israel.
Nevertheless, they didn't depart from the Jeroboam's case,
Hence making the rest of Israel sin the more.

Now, the wooden image also remained in Samaria.
Along with the army of Jehoahaz.
Only fifty horsemen, ten chariots,
And ten-thousand-foot soldiers.
Were assigned by the King of Syria,
To destroy and make them like the dust at threshing.

The rest of the acts of Jehoahaz,
All that he did, and his might,
Are written in the book of the chronicles.
Detailing the kings of Israel,
And how they'd fight?

Thus, Jehoahaz rested with his fathers,
Was buried in Samaria in haste.

So that Joash his son, could reign in his place.

In the thirty-seventh year of Joash's rule over Judah,
Jehoash the son of Jehoahaz became king over Israel in Samaria.
Jehoash went on to reign for sixteen years.
Doing evil in the sight of the LORD as his fathers did.

Now the rest of the acts of Joash,
From all the sins he committed,
Along with the demonstration to kill Syria three times quickly,
Instead of following Elisha's command - being six times at least.
To the fight he had with Amaziah,
Who was leading Judah as the King.
Indeed, all records for Joash, are written,
And can be found in the book of chronicles the same.
For it is living proof that Joash was king,
Not for God's will, but for personal gain.

Following Joash's burial in Samaria with the kings of Israel.
Elisha the prophet had died,
Thus, the Israelites who were faithful in the Lord,
Took heed to bury him in one accord.

Before the burial of the man of God- Elisha,
A raiding Moabite band, in the spring of that year,
Invaded Israel slyly, to plan an attack.
So it was, as the Israelites were burying Elisha,
That suddenly band of raiders nearby.
Placed one of the injured in the tomb of Elisha- to die.
But when the man was let down and touched Elisha's bones,
He was revived and stood on his feet- alone.

Hazael king of Syria oppressed Israel all the days of Jehoahaz' life.
But the LORD remained gracious and compassionate on the Israelites.

Regarding and comforting them during their oppression.
Thereby keeping His covenant with Father Abraham, Isaac, and Jacob, alive.

Fortunately, after Hazael king of Syria finally died,
Ben—Hadad his son, was assigned to reign.
Indeed, during this time Jehoash the son of Jehoahaz took a chance.
Defeating Ben Hadad three consecutive times,
And recapturing the cities of Israel, from his hands.

The Reigns Of Amaziah And Jeroboam Iii (Ref: 2 Kings, Chapter 14)

In the second year of Joash the son of Jehoahaz
Amaziah the son of Joash, king of Judah, became king.
Amaziah was twenty-five years old at that time,
And reigned over Jerusalem for several years-twenty-nine.

Amaziah's mother's -Jehoaddan, served the Lord's name,
Brought up Amaziah in Jerusalem, to do the same.

Yet, the high places were not taken away,
So, the people still sacrificed and burned incense there.

Now, as the kingdom was established in his hand,
Amaziah went on to fulfil the Law of Moses, that stands,
"Fathers shall not be put to death for their children,
Nor shall children be put to death for their fathers.
But a person shall be put to death for his sin alone".
Therefore, Amaziah ordered for his servants for execution,
As it turned out, they murdered his father- the former king.

Then Amaziah sent messengers to Jehoash to say,
"Come, let us face one another in battle today".

In reply, Jehoash king of Israel said,
"The thistle that was in Lebanon,

Has been sent to the cedar.
Thus, give your daughter,
So that my son can have her as a wife.
Like a wild beast in Lebanon, passed by and trampled the thistle.
You have indeed defeated Edom, and your heart has been lifted.
Glory in that and stay at your home.
For why should you meddle with trouble alone? "

Therefore, Jehoash king of Israel went out to fight.
And face Amaziah king of Judah, for another time.
The kings faced one another at Beth Shemesh,
A place that belonged to Judah.

Thus, Judah was defeated by Israel in the end,
Leaving every man fleeing back to his tent.
Then Jehoash king of Israel captured Amaziah at Beth Shemesh.
While breaking down the four-hundred-cubit gate, at Ephraim.

In addition, Amaziah took all hostages and returned to Samaria,
With gold, silver and articles that were found,
Including all the treasuries from the king's house.

Now the rest of the acts of Jehoash which he did,
His might, and how he fought with Amaziah- Judah's king.
Are not written in the book of the chronicles of the Israel kings?
Thus, Jehoash rested with his fathers,
And at Samaria, was buried with the kings of Israel.

Jeroboam his son reigned in Jehoash's place.
Amaziah the son of Joash, king of Judah,
Lived for another fifteen years- after Jehoash's death,
And was victim of a conspiracy.

This conspiracy against Amaziah, rooted from Jerusalem,
Yet, as Amaziah fled to Lachish;
He ended up dying there,

From a set of perverse persons.

Amaziah's corpse was brought on horses to be buried,
At Jerusalem with his fathers, in the City of David.
And all the people of Judah took Azariah- a sixteen-year-old,
To become king, instead of his father Amaziah.

Azariah built Elath
And restored it to Judah,
And when it was the fifteenth year of Amaziah's reign over Judah,
Azariah rested with his fathers- as what was due.
Hence, Jeroboam the son of Joash, became the new king,
Reigning over Israel and Samaria, for forty-one years.

Alas, Jeroboam did evil in the sight of the LORD.
And didn't part from all the sins of Jeroboam.
Fortunately, he restored the territory of Israel.
From the entrance of Hamath,
To the Sea of the Arabah.
Fulfilling the word of the Lord,
Spoken through His servant Jonah- the son of Amittai,
And a prophet who was from Gath Hepher.

Now, as the LORD saw Israel's bitter afflictions- bond and free,
The Lord knew he had to send a helper for Israel to see.
The Lord would not blot out the name of Israel- despite their sins,
Hence, he continued to save them by the hand of Jeroboam.

Now the rest of the acts of Jeroboam,
All that he did— his might, how he made war,
To how he recaptured for Israel,
Damascus and Hamath- belonged to Judah.
Are written in the book of the chronicles,

Detailing his kingship, triumphs before his son- Zechariah,
Was summoned to reign in his place.

Right Vs Evil in The Lord's Sight (Ref: 2 Kings, Chapter 15)

In the twenty-seventh year of Jeroboam king of Israel,
Azariah the son of Amaziah, king of Judah, became king.
He was sixteen years old when he became king,
And reigned over Jerusalem for fifty-two years.

His mother's name was Jecholiah of Jerusalem.
So, as his mother was upright, Azariah was too,
Thereby, committed to doing what was right,
In the sight of the LORD and the Israelite people.

Yet, the high places were not removed.
Prompting some people to sacrifice and burn incense there.
In consequence, the LORD struck Azariah with leprosy,
That made him stay isolated from all,
And prompting Jotham his son,
To look over the royal house,
As well as judge the people of the land.

Now the rest of the acts of Azariah,
And all that he did and did not do,
Are written in the book of the chronicles for you.

Nevertheless, when Azariah eventually died,
He was buried with his fathers in the City of David.
Allowing Jotham his son, to officially reign in his place.

In the thirty-eighth year of Azariah king of Judah,
Zechariah the son of Jeroboam reigned.
His reign was over Israel in Samaria,
And continued for six months.

Zechariah did evil in the sight of the LORD,
No better or worse as his fathers had done.
Hence, he did not depart from the sins of Jeroboam- son of Nebat,
Making the people of Israel stumble again in sin.

By God's will, Shallum the son of Jabesh conspired,
And then killed Zechariah in front of the people's eyes.
Following this devised and terrible killing that occurred,
Shallum reigned as king- although no one concurred.

This was the word of the LORD,
Which He spoke to Jehu, saying,
"Your sons shall sit on the throne of Israel,
To the fourth generation as well".

Shallum the son of Jabesh,
Was the king in the thirty-ninth year,
While Uzziah king of Judah,
Reigned in Samaria for a month.

Menahem- son of Gadi, went from Tirzah to Samaria,
To strike Shallum the son of Jabesh,
And reign as king in his place.

Now the rest of the acts of Shallum,
And the conspiracy which he led,
Are written in the book of the chronicles.
As all of Israel's former kings and men.

Then from Tirzah, Menahem attacked Tiphsah,
Thus, all people there, and its territories, were ripped open.
Being the thirty-ninth year of Azariah king of Judah,
Menahem the son of Gadi became king over Israel.
Reigning a total of ten years in Samaria.
Menahem did evil in the sight of the LORD.

Thus, as Menahem didn't depart from the sins of Jeroboam,
Pul king of Assyria came against the land.
So, Menahem gave Pul a thousand talents of silver,
To stop his warfare plans.

It is important to note that the thousand talents of silver,
Came from wealthy men in Israel.
Yes, Menahem collected fifty shekels of silver from every man,
To round up to the thousand talents of silver, given to Pul's hands.

Fortunately, with this large sum of silver,
Pul-the king of Assyria turned back from creating harm.
Leaving the land and people of Israel,
No longer alarmed.

Now the rest of the acts of Menahem,
And all that he did,
Are written in the book of the chronicles,
Like all the previous Israel kings.

So Menahem rested with his fathers,
Before Pekahiah his son reigned in his place.
It was then the fiftieth year of Azariah king of Judah,
When Pekahiah the son of Menahem ruled over Israel in Samaria.

Pekahiah reigned as king for only two years,
Committing evils in the sight of the Lord.
Then Pekah the son of Remaliah, an officer of his,
Conspired against him in Samaria,
Before killing him there in the citadel of his house.
Nevertheless, as Argob and Arieh were there,
Pekah killed them, and fifty men of Gilead.

Now the rest of the acts of Pekahiah,
And all that he did before he was murdered,

Are written in the book of the chronicles,
As before mentioned.

It was in the fifty-second year of Azariah king of Judah's reign,
When Pekah the son of Remaliah became king over Israel.
Like Pekahiah, he reigned over Israel and Samaria,
Reigning a long twenty years- doing evil in the sight of the LORD.

Hence, Tiglath-Pileser king of Assyria came and took,
Ijon, Abel Beth Maachah, Janoah,
Along with Kedesh, Hazor, Gilead, and Galilee.
Making all the land his – Naphtali.

Tiglath then carried these peoples captive- to Assyria.
Before Hoshea- Elah's son, led a conspiracy against him there.
The conspiracy involved Pekah the son of Remaliah to get up and kill,
Tiglath, before taking over as king in his place.

In the second year of Pekah the son of Remaliah,
Jotham the son of Uzziah, king of Judah, began to reign.
Jotham was twenty-five years old when he became king,
And he reigned for sixteen years in Jerusalem.

Jotham's mother's name was Jerusha.
Who was the daughter of Zadok.
Hence, thanks to his good mother,
Jotham did what was right in the sight of the LORD.

Yet, the high places were not removed during Jotham's time.
Allowing the people of Israel, to burn incense there and make idol sacrifice.
Nevertheless, Jotham built the Upper Gate,
To encompass the house of the LORD- in one place.

Now the rest of the acts of Jotham,
And all that he did,

Are written in the book of the chronicles,
Like the previous kings over Judah, once did.

In those days the LORD began to send Rezin king of Syria,
Along with Pekah the son of Remaliah,
To go against Judah, before Jotham rested,
And was buried with his fathers.
Prompting Ahaz his son, to reign in his place.

Ahaz' Compromise (Ref: 2 Kings, Chapter 16)

In the seventeenth year of Pekah's reign,
Ahaz the son of Jotham, king of Judah, came.
Before being appointed as Jerusalem's new king.

Ahaz ruled over the people for several years-sixteen.
Fulfilling his own desires, not the Lord's by any means.
Thus, Rezin king of Syria and Pekah, came to make war,
With Jerusalem and besieged Ahaz unlike before.

So, at that time, Rezin captured Elath for Syria,
Also driving the men of Judah from Elath.
Then the Edomites went to Elath.
And dwell there, to this day.

Yet, Rezin could not overcome Ahaz,
For Ahaz sent messengers to save him.
Thus, the messengers of Ahaz, took silver and gold.
To gift Rezin as a peace offering and reward.

Rezin readily accepted this gift from the house of the Lord,
Thereby freeing Ahaz to his messengers, in one accord.
Ahaz, now free, decided to go up against Damascus,
Taking its' people captive, all the way to Kir.

Following Ahaz's success in Damascus,
He then skilfully killed Rezin.

After this, King Ahaz went to Tiglath-Pileser.
While discussing his plans with the king of Assyria,
Ahaz saw an altar that he hadn't seen before,
And so, he sent Urijah the priest,
To get the pattern and design of the altar.

As Urijah wrote the altar workmanship- to the tea,
Urijah built an altar for King Ahaz from Damascus, accordingly.
Indeed, it was when king Ahaz returned from Damascus,
That he saw the wonderful altar with offerings on it.

So, King Ahaz offered a burnt and grain offering,
With a poured drink and sprinkle of blood.
He also brought the bronze altar before the LORD,
From the front of the temple, between the new altars.
And the revered house of the LORD.

Later placing the altar on the north side,
King Ahaz commanded Urijah to do the time.
Hence, Urijah burnt the morning burnt offering,
The evening grain offering,
Along with the king's burnt sacrifice.
In addition, Urijah offered the king's grain offering,
With the burnt offering,
On behalf of the people circumcised.
Likewise drink offerings and the sprinkle of blood was made,
To symbolise the burnt offering
And the blood of animal sacrifices laid.

Certainly, the bronze altar was for King Ahaz to have God bless,
Thus, Urijah the priest, followed the king's orders- for the best.

King Ahaz then cut off the panels of the carts,
Removing the lavers apart.
And he took down the Sea- from the bronze oxen under it,
To put on a pavement of stones over it.

At the same token, he removed the Sabbath pavilion,
Along with the outer entrance from the house of the LORD.
Because of the king of Assyria.

Now the rest of the acts of Ahaz,
Are written in the book of the chronicles,
Detailing his time as a king over Judah.
So, as Ahaz rested with his fathers,
And at the City of David was buried,
Hezekiah his son, took over in haste,
As the rightful king in his place.

An Israel Invasion (Ref: 2 Kings, Chapter 17)

In the twelfth year of Ahaz king of Judah,
Hoshea-son of Elah became the king of Israel in Samaria.
Hoshea, he reigned for a total of nine years.
Doing evil in the sight of the LORD,
Fulfilling all his lusts- doing whatever he pleased.

Shalmaneser king of Assyria came up against him.
As Hoshea became his vassal, and paid tribute money.
Moreover, the king of Assyria uncovered a conspiracy by Hoshea
For he had sent messengers to the king of Egypt.

The messengers brought no tribute to the king of Assyria,
Defying the traditions that were done year by year.
Therefore, the king of Assyria shut Hoshea up.
Bounding him a terribly dark prison.

Now the king of Assyria went throughout all the land,
Travelling all the way up to Samaria.
Thereby besieging it for three years.

By the ninth year of Hoshea's reign,
The king of Assyria took Samaria and carried Israel away.

Israel was carried away to Assyria, and placed in Halah,
By the Habor, the River of Gozan,
As well as the cities of the Medes.

For so it was that the children of Israel sinned,
Despite the Lord previously saving them,
From the Pharoah- king of Egypt.

Thus, as the children of Israel built a watchtower,
To fortified cities with high places to burn incense to idols,
The Lord was provoked to anger for their devices.
Hence, the Lord pleaded to them, "You shall not do this thing".
Yet the people of Israel, refused to concede.

Nevertheless, as the people of Israel wouldn't adhere,
To the Lord's plea or commands,
The Lord was left heartbroken again.

To make matters worse, the Lord witnessed them making,
A moulded image, with two calves named Baal to worship,
Along with soothsaying and witchcraft.
Undoubtedly, this provoked the Lord to anger,
On top of His very broken heart.

Therefore, the LORD rejected all the descendants of Israel,
Allowing them to be afflicted and delivered out,
To the plunderers and enemies all around.

Then He tore Israel from the house of David,
Leaving them to be carried away to Assyria.
Then the king of Assyria brought people from all places.
From Babylon, Cuthah, Ava,
To Hamath and Sepharvaim.

Likewise, the king of Assyria placed the Israelites.
In the cities of Samaria,
Prompting the Lord to send out lions.

The lions killed some of the Israelites,
Proving that there was punishment for those,
Who did not commit the rituals of God,
In front of the people or the land.

Then the king of Assyria commanded, saying,
"Send there one of the priests whom you brought.
Let him go and dwell there.
Indeed, may this priest teach them the rituals,
Of the God of the Israelites' land".

Hence, one of the priests whom they had carried away,
Came and dwelt in Bethel,
To teach everyone to way.
He taught those who would listen,
On how to fear the Lord.
And commit the rituals fitting,
As much as pleasing, to the Lord.

Nonetheless, the priest's efforts weren't enough,
As every nation continued to make their false gods.
For instance, the men of Babylon made Succoth Benoth,
The men of Cuth made Nergal,
The men of Hamath made Ashima,
The Avites made Nibhaz and Tartak;
Even the Sepharvites went as far as to burn their own children.
To add on this shameful thing,
The Sepharvites made new false gods:
Named Adrammelech and Anammelech.

What a contradiction is this?
For the people and nations learned how to fear the Lord.
Yet continued to serve false gods.

To this day the descendants of these nations,
Continue practicing the former rituals.

And keep on following their own lustful desires,
Taking no interest in fearing or following the true Lord.

Hezekiah's Reigh, Assyria's Threat (Ref: 2 Kings, Chapter 18)

Now it came to pass in the third year,
That the son of Elah- Hosea,
Was summoned king over Israel.
Leaving Hezekiah- son of Ahaz,
To rule over as king over Judah.

Hezekiah was only twenty-five years old,
When summoned as the king of Judah.
Hezekiah reigned for twenty-nine years,
Strengthening Judah along with Jerusalem.

Hezekiah's mother's name was Abi.
Who was the daughter Zechariah,
And thereby loved the Lord dearly.

Thus, Hezekiah was brought up to do what was right,
Fulfilling the Lord's commandments,
Along with fulfilling what his father David had done.

Hezekiah went the extra mile to,
Remove the high places,
To breaking the sacred pillars too.

Hezekiah also cut down the wooden images,
Broke in the pieces of the bronze serpent- during Moses' time,
There, terminating the history behind that serpent- Nehushtan,
Which had made the Israelites burn incense to it and die.

Indeed, Hezekiah trusted in the LORD God of Israel,
Unlike any king over Judah- before or after him.

For he held fast to the LORD and did not depart at all.
Abiding from commandments from Moses' time,
Thereby only pleasing the Lord.

Certainly, in return for Hezekiah's love and trust in the Lord,
The Lord was with him for always.
Hence, Hezekiah prospered wherever he'd go.

From when he rebelled against the king of Assyria,
Because the king did not serve God, nor live uprightly.
To when he subdued the Philistines,
As far as Gaza and its territory,
Along with a watchtower to fortified city.

Now it came to pass in the fourth year,
Of King Hezekiah's great reign,
That Hoshea the son of Elah, king of Israel,
With Shalmaneser king of Assyria came.

These two kings came up against Samaria- besieging it.
So, at the end of three years of fighting,
The two kings finally took it.

In the sixth year of Hezekiah, Samaria was taken,
Hence, making the ninth year of Hoshea's reign,
A nightmare in every way.

Indeed, the king of Assyria carried Israel away captive,
Putting them in Halah,
To then by the Habor,
River of Gozan,
All the way to the cities of the Medes.

All of this happened to Israel as a wakeup call.
For they continued to transgress

Commit sin and stray away from the Lord.
Truly, all the directions that Moses had ensured,
And commanded them to follow.
Were disregarded as nothing more.

Now, in the fourteenth year of King Hezekiah's reign,
Sennacherib king of Assyria came up against all- again.
From all the fortified cities of Judah,
He took and raided.
Prompting Hezekiah king of Judah,
To send a letter pleading for peace like before.

Hence, the letter moved the king of Assyria at Lachish, to say,
"I have done wrong; turn away from me.
Whatever you impose on me I will pay."

Following the king of Assyria's assessing the King of Judah,
A total of three hundred talents of silver
As well as thirty talents of gold,
Was given to make King Hezekiah.

Then the king of Assyria sent the Tartan,
The Rabsaris, along with the Rabshakeh from Lachish.
And used all these people,
To form a great army.

The army was made to go against Jerusalem.
Thus, the army stood from the upper pool,
On the highway to the Fuller's Field
And by the aqueduct.

Nevertheless, when they called for King Hezekiah,
Eliakim the son of Hilkiah
Who was over the household,
As well as Shebna the scribe,
And Joah the son of Asaph,
Came out to help plan a fight.

Following these courses of events,
The King of Assyria- Rabshakeh, said to them,

"What confidence is this in which you trust?
You speak of having plans and power for war; as such?
But you Eliakim, Shebna, and Joah,
Bark more than it bites.
And you aim to rebel against me in spite?"

"What is more,
You are trusting in the staff of this broken reed- Egypt,
On which if a man leans,
It will go into his hand and pierce it.
And so is Pharaoh king of Egypt, to all who trust in him.
But if you say you trust in the LORD,
It is not He high places and whose altars, Hezekiah has destroyed?"

After orating this huge speech,
The King of Assyria began to proclaim:
"Now therefore, I urge you to give a pledge,
And I will give you two thousand horses in return".

At first, Eliakim the son of Hilkiah,
Along with Shebna, and Joah,
Could not understand the words spoken,
So, they asked Rabshakeh to ask his servants to help.
And indeed, the servants translated the message into Aramaic.

Then as Rabshakeh stood and called out saying,
"Hear the word of the great king,
Do not let Hezekiah deceive you,
For he shall not be able to deliver you,
So, make peace with me".

The whole gist of Rabshakeh's words,
Made the people feel wrongly prepared.

For the people were deceived to believe,
That in return of disobeying the Lord and Hezekiah's words,
They would receive a land filled with grain, wine, bread,
As well as vineyards, olive groves, and honey.

With clothes now torn from the people's wrath,
Eliakim the son of Hilkiah, Shebna the scribe and Joah the son of Asaph,
Determined to keep strong while delivering the news to Hezekiah,
In hopes that the truth of the matter, would be intact.

God Delivers Jerusalem from Assyria (Ref: 2 Kings, Chapter 19)

When King Hezekiah heard terrible news,
He tore his clothes, covered himself in sack clothes,
To pray for sweet refuge,
Into the house of the LORD.

Following this, he sent for Eliakim through,
Along with Shebna the scribe, and elderly priests.
Whom all wore sack clothes,
Joining Hezekiah in prayer too.

"This day is a day of trouble, and rebuke,
A day of blasphemy for the children.
May the Lord hear all the words of the Rabshakeh,
Whom the king of Assyria has sent reproach to the Living God".

Indeed, the servants of King Hezekiah came to Isaiah.
And Isaiah said to them the following words,
"Thus says the LORD: "Do not be afraid of what you have heard.
For surely, I will send a spirit upon him- a rumour,
And thereby return to his own land".

Following this declaration from the Lord,
Rabshakeh found the king of Assyria and returned.

As he returned, he warred against Libnah for he heard.
That Libnah had departed from Lachish.

Despite the kings of Assyria, being destroyed,
Hezekiah took a letter with him.
Then when he spread it before the LORD.
He began to weep and utter a prayer from within.

After Hezekiah prayed before the LORD,
Declaring His divinity on Heaven and Earth,
The Lord was inclined to listen to him,
And thereby heal his visible hurt.

So it was that the One who dwells between the cherubim,
And Who destroyed the false gods from the Assyrian kings.
Sent Isaiah- the son of Amoz, to comfort Hezekiah and say:
"Thus says the LORD God of Israel today".
For because you have prayed to him,
And against Sennacherib king of Assyria,
He will heed to your heartful request,
And has promised this concerning him:

'The virgin, the daughter of Zion,
Has despised you, laughed you to scorn.
The daughter of Jerusalem
Has shaken her head behind your back- torn!

'Whom have you reproached?
Against whom have you raised your voice,
And lifted your eyes on high hopes?
Against the Holy One of Israel- bad choice.

By your messengers you have reproached the Lord,
And said: "By the multitude of my chariots.
I have come up to the height of the mountain ford.

To the limits of Lebanon.
I will cut down its tall cedars as I please.
And its choice cypress trees.

I will enter the extremity of its borders,
To its fruitful forest so dense.
I have dug and drunk strange water.
With the soles of my feet, I have dried up.
All the brooks of defence."

'Did you not hear in the past,
How I made it hard,
From ancient times
To this time.

For crushing fortified cities into heaps of ruins.
Will have inhabitants with little power.
So, they dismayed and confounded.
Will be as the grass of the field- grounded.

They shall be like the green herb,
As the grass on the housetops
As well as grain blighted there,
Before it is grown across.

'But I know your dwelling place,
Your going out and coming in,
And your rage against Me,
Though you were the committer of sin.

Hence, your rage against Me and your tumult
Have come up to My ears and eyes,
Therefore, I will put My hook in your nose.
And My bridle in your lips, this time.

I will turn you back.
By the way which you came.
'This shall be a sign to you:
And for all who put me to shame.

You shall eat this year such as grows of itself,
As for the second year the same.
Also, in the third year you will sow and reap,
Plant vineyards and eat the fruit of them plain.

The remnant that escaped of the house of Judah
Shall again take root downward,
And bear fruit upward.
For out of Jerusalem shall go a remnant,
Which escape from Mount Zion.

Indeed, the zeal of the LORD of hosts will do this.'
He shall not come into this city,
Nor shoot an arrow there,
Nor come before it with shield.

Nor shall He build a siege mound against it.
By the way that he came,
By the same shall he return.
And he shall not come into this city again.

'For I will defend this city, to save it and its' people,
For My own sake and for My servant David,
Along with the descendants that are his equal.

It came to pass on a certain night,
That the angel of the LORD went out,
Killing in the camp of the Assyrians
One hundred and eighty-five thousand all about.

So, when people arose early in the morning,
They saw terrible corpses— all dead.
Making Sennacherib king of Assyria,
To depart quickly- in full torment.

Now it came to pass, as Sennacherib was worshipping,
In the Nineveh temple of Nisroch- an idol.
That his sons Adrammelech and Sharezer,
Struck him down with the sword- left for dead.

Thus, following this unfortunate turn of events,
Esarhaddon – Sennacherib's son.
Was summoned up,
To reign in his place.

Time to Die (Ref: 2 Kings, Chapter 20)

In those days Hezekiah was sick,
So, Isaiah, the son of Amoz, went and said to him,
"Thus says the LORD: 'Set your house in order,
For you shall die tomorrow".

At this prophecy, Hezekiah turned his face,
And stood up against the wall to pray.
He prayed to the Lord to show him mercy,
And then went out to weep bitterly.

So, it happened before Isaiah had gone away,
That the word of Lord came to him saying,
"Return and tell Hezekiah- the leader of My people,
That I have heard his prayers and seen his tears.
And on the third day, I shall surely heal him too".

With that Isaiah boiled a lump of figs,
Before placing it on Hezekiah's face and limbs.
Indeed, it was as the Lord said and planned,
For Hezekiah to recover and resume to his duties on hand.

Berodach-Baladan along with the King of Babylon too,
Sent Hezekiah letters to congratulate his recovery through.
In repay for their kind regards and open care,
Hezekiah invited them to his house to share.

Hence, Hezekiah showed and shared his treasures afoot,
From silver, gold, spices, armoury, and precious ointments too.
Indeed, there was nothing in his house or in all his dominion,
That Hezekiah did not show and share through.

Then Isaiah the prophet went to King Hezekiah, to say,
"Where did these men come and speak?
So, Hezekiah said, "They came from a far country, from Babylon.
They came with love and committed me no wrong.
So, I showed and shared with them the treasures of my house,
To thank them for sending me letters,
And for being so kind".

Then Isaiah said to Hezekiah, the following,
"Hear the word of the LORD coming.
For behold, all that was in your house,
Along with what your fathers accumulated too.
Shall be carried to Babylon.
Until nothing shall be left for you".

So, Hezekiah said to Isaiah,
"The word you have spoken is good!
For at least there'll be peace in my days?"

Now the rest of the acts of Hezekiah- all his might.
From how he made a pool and a tunnel
That brought water too,
His city and the people all over,
Ensuring all had water and kept well.

After the fifteen years had passed,
King Hezekiah rested with his fathers at last.

Leaving Manasseh his son alone,
And thereby take over the throne.

Bad to The Bone (Ref: 2 Kings, Chapter 21)

Manasseh was twelve years old,
When he became king.
And thanks to his mother- Hephzibah,
He did evil throughout his reign.

Alas, he did evil for all fifty-five years of his reign,
Making the Lord upset from abominations again.
From building the high places that Hezekiah his father had destroyed.
To raising up the altars and giving incense to false idols such as Baal.

Certainly, Manasseh followed the way of Ahab- a former king,
Hence leading the people of Israel to all fall into sin.
He then built altars in the image of the idol- Asherah, too.
Thereby polluting the Lord's house, all through.

If this wasn't evil enough, Manasseh ordered for his own son,
To pass through the fire, practice soothsaying and use witchcraft.
On top of this, he consulted spiritisms and mediums- taboo,
Thereby provoking God to anger too.

Yet, no one paid any attention to God's commands,
Hence, leaving Manasseh to seduce all over the land.
Then the Lord spoke, by His servants the prophets, saying,

"As Manasseh has done these abominations.
I shall bring calamity upon Jerusalem and Judah.
So, whoever hears of it, let their ears tingle.
For I will stretch over Jerusalem and all the people.
Indeed, I will wipe Jerusalem as one wipes a dish,
Wiping it and turning it upside down to the sink.
To add, I will forsake the remnant of My inheritance.
And deliver them into to their enemies- as remnant".

The Lord proclaimed this punishment as Manasseh made.
All the people sin more since their forefathers left Egypt away.
Moreover, as Manasseh shed innocent blood everywhere,
God ensured that Manasseh's punishment would be bare.

Now the rest of the acts of Manasseh— all that he did,
Along with the evil and sin that he committed.
Are written in the book of the chronicles,
As did all the kings of Judah before him.

So, Manasseh rested with his father's burial space.
This burial space was at his house garden- Uzza.
And after he was quickly buried there,
His son Amon reigned in his place.
Now Amon was twenty-two years old at the time,
Being a decent age to reign as king in line.
However, he reigned for only two years,
And kept doing as he pleased.

Amon's mother's name was Meshullemeth.
She was the daughter of Haruz of Jotbah,
And advised Amon to be like his father Manasseh,
Thereby, making him a faithless king- up to no good.

So it was that Amon he walked in Manasseh's ways,
Serving idols, worshipping them,
To cursing the Lord by his actions- everyday.

Nevertheless, it was not long before his servants conspired.
To kill him, which they did, and took over his family's pride.

Following Ammon's death, the people of the land took revenge.
Hence, killing all the people who played a part in his death,

Now, the rest of the acts of Amon- a disgrace,
Are written in the book of the chronicles too.

So, after he was buried in the garden of Uzza- in his tomb,
His only son- Josiah, reigned in his place.

King Josiah, Great King (Ref: 2 Kings, Chapter 22)

Josiah was eight years old when he became king,
And he reigned over Jerusalem, for thirty-one years.

His mother's name was Jedidah.
A daughter of Adaiah of Bozkath.
And thanks to his mother's grace,
Josiah followed God, all his days.

Now it came to pass, in the eighteenth year,
That King Josiah, sent Shaphan the scribe;
Along with the son of Azaliah,
And the son of Meshullam.

After sending these people to the Lord's house,
The Lord's voice announced:
"Go up to Hilkiah the high priest,
So that he may count the money.
For the doorkeepers have gathered donations to give,
To those doing the work as they live".

As the Lord said, Hilkiah initiated the roles out,
For people to repair the damages of the Lord's house.
So it was that carpenters and builders and masons.
Bought timber and hewn stone to repair changes.

Then Hilkiah the high priest said to Shaphan the scribe,
"I have found the Book of the Law this time".
Following this, Hilkiah gave the book to Shaphan to read it,
And thereby, making accounts of the work committed.

Now it happened, when the king heard,
That he tore his clothes until he was bare.

Then the king commanded Hilkiah the priest,
For Ahikam the son of Shaphan,
Achbor the son of Michaiah,
Shaphan the scribe, and Asaiah a servant of the king.

So Hilkiah the priest, Ahikam, Achbor,
To Shaphan, and Asaiah,
Went to Huldah the prophetess- wife of Shallum.

As they spoke with her, she said to them,

"Thus says the LORD God of Israel again,
Tell the man who sent you to Me,
That I will bring calamity.
Indeed, my wrath shall be aroused, not quenched.
Against the people and this place.

But as for the king of Judah,
Who sent you to inquire,
I will state that as his heart was tender,
He and his people, will not die.
In fact, the people of Judah, will be gathered in peace,
And therefore, not see Israel's planned calamities".

Josiah's Leadership (Ref: 2 Kings, Chapter 23)

The elders of Judah and Jerusalem were gathered to.
See the king and his inhabitants too.
As the elders read in their hearing, of all the words found,
The king listened to the Book of the Covenant, feeling astound.

Following this, the king stood by a pillar in peace.
To create a new Covenant with the Lord- to keep.
Indeed, all the people took a stand for the covenant.
Thereby following the model of Hilkiah, the high priest.

So, it was with Hilkiah leading the priests of the second order-in accord,
That the doorkeepers, brought out of the temple, of the LORD.
Furthermore, all the wicked high priests and perverted persons faced.
A punishment for burning incense to those idols in place.
Following that, the articles made for Baal and Asherah, were removed.
Leaving space for Hilkiah to lead the new.

Then Hilkiah removed the horses,
At the entrance to the house of the LORD.
By the chamber of Nathan-Melech- the officer who was in the court.

Not long after, he burned the chariots of the sun with fire.
So that the altars that were on the roof were dire.
Following that, the upper chamber of Ahaz,
Along with the sacred pillars, were cut down.

Moreover, the altar that was at Bethel,
Beside the high places that made Israel sin,
Were broke down, burned, and crushed to powder,
Leaving tombs stuck up on the mountains.

As Josiah turned, he sent and took the bones,
Out of the tombs and burned them on the altar for atone.
Then Josiah said, "What gravestone is this that I see?"
So, the men of the city, informed him readily.

Certainly, the men said the following facts.
On how the tomb was of the man of God.
Who had come from Judah and proclaimed the truth.

After listening intently, Josiah decided that,
The prophet's bones would be safe and intact.
In addition, Josiah ordered executions of all the priests,
Who burned men's bones on them as strange offerings.

Josiah commanded his people to keep the Passover.
To fulfil their Covenant to the LORD.
And so it was that in the eighteenth year of King Josiah's reign.
That the Passover was held before the LORD in Jerusalem's plains.

Moreover, Josiah put away those who consulted mediums and spiritists,
Including all the household gods and idols that created abominations.
Certainly, before Josiah, there was not one king,
Who had turned to the LORD with all his heart,
With all his soul, and with all his might,
And with all his being.

In Josiah's days of kingship
The Pharaoh Necho went.
To the aid of the king of Assyria,
To the River Euphrates.
And King Josiah went against to win.
Thereby defeating, and eventually killing him.

Now the rest of the acts of Josiah,
And all that he did,
Are they not written in the book of the chronicles,
Just like all the previous Judah kings?

So it was, that after King Josiah passed away,
That Jehoahaz, twenty-three years old, took his place.
Alas, Jehoahaz reigned for only three months.
Doing evil in the sight of the Lord at once.

Jehoahaz' mother's name was Hamutal;
She was the daughter of Jeremiah of Libnah.
Hence, she encouraged him to do evil,
According to what his forefathers had done.

Now Pharaoh Necho put him in prison at Riblah,

So that he mightn't reign of Jerusalem any longer.
Then, he imposed on the land a tribute to be:
One hundred talents of silver and a talent of gold to keep.

After Jehoahaz' expected death,
Pharaoh Necho made Eliakim reign instead.
Now, Eliakim was another son of the late Josiah.
And he changed his name to Jehoiakim,
Before going up to Egypt- where he eventually died.

Judah Subjected Under Babylon (Ref: 2 Kings, Chapter 24)

In the days that Nebuchadnezzar was king,
Babylon lived comfortably for three years.
Also, Jehoiakim became his vassal for all that time.
Before turning against him in a crime.

On top of betrayal, the LORD also sent,
A raiding band of Chaldeans, bands of Syrians,
Bands of Moabites, and a bands of Ammon men.
All went against Judah to destroy it.
Thereby fulfilling the word of the Lord,
Spoken by the prophets again.

Clearly, the Lord executed justice on Jerusalem,
For Manasseh and Nebuchadnezzar, shed innocent blood.

Now the rest of the acts of Jehoiakim,
And all that he did,
Are written in the book of the chronicles,
As before was did.

Sooner or later, Jehoiakim rested in his forefathers' burial site.
Leaving Jehoiachin his son to reign over with might.
For instance, since Jehoiachin's reign began,

The king of Egypt did not come out of his land.
Furthermore, being the king of Babylon by fate,
Jehoiachin took treasures from Egypt from the Brook,
To the River Euphrates.

Jehoiachin committed great things as king,
Albeit for any eighteen-year-old.
Yet, he reigned over Jerusalem for just three months.

Now, Jehoiachin's mother's name was Nehushta.
She was the daughter of Elnathan of Jerusalem.
As a result, he was advised to do evil.
Thereby causing a stumble for all the Lord's people.

At that time, the servants of Nebuchadnezzar besieged the city,
And Nebuchadnezzar, carried the treasures out as he pleased.
Then, he cut in pieces all the articles of gold,
Which Solomon king of Israel had made for the Lord.

What is more, he carried all captains, craftsmen, and smiths,
Into a captivity for their service and workmanship.
All in all, Nebuchadnezzar made no sense,
As he punished people who were godly- innocent.

Finally, this infamous king of Babylon, made,
Mattaniah, Jehoiachin's uncle, reign as king in his place.
The first thing Mattaniah initiated in his rule,
Was the changing of his name to Zedekiah- how cool.

Thus, Zedekiah was twenty-one years of age.
And reigned as king for eleven years,
Indeed, those were evil days.

All in all, because of the anger of the LORD was tremendous,
The Israelites were finally cast out from His presence.
And as a way for Zedekiah to revel in this tragedy,

He rebelled against the Babylonian king.

Jerusalem's Fall, Israel's Captivity (Ref: 2 Kings, Chapter 25)

Now it came to pass, in the ninth year of Nebuchadnezzar's reign,
That his army came and encamped over Jerusalem.
Indeed, the city was besieged until the eleventh year of King Zedekiah.
And by the ninth day of the fourth month, the famine had become dire.

Thanks to the famine, there was no food for the people of the land.
And with the city wall broken through,
All the men of war fled the land.

Then, the army of the Chaldeans pursued the king,
Before finally overtaking his army as well as him.
Following that, the Chaldeans killed Zedekiah's sons- before his eyes,
Before bounding Zedekiah, himself, with bronze fetters, at all sides.

Indeed, in the nineteenth year of King Nebuchadnezzar's reign,
Nebuzaradan the captain of the guard, came to Jerusalem again.
Nebuzaradan burned the house of the LORD and the king's house.
Along with the houses and walls of Jerusalem- all around.

Then Nebuzaradan the captain of the guard carried away captives.
These captives were people who remained in Jerusalem.
Yet, he showed mercy to the poor of the land-vinedressers and farmers.
Thereby giving them a chance to be no longer under arms.

Regarding the house of the Lord and its' experience of looting,
It is important to note that the bronze pillars and gold were taken.
On top of this, pots, shovels, trimmers, spoons, and all bronze utensils,
Were taken to prevent the priests to use for their work.
And if that wasn't enough, the Chaldeans took all things silver and gold,

From the two pillars- one Sea, and the carts.
Which Solomon had made for the house of the LORD.

Finally, the captain Nebuzaradan, took Seraiah the chief priest,
Along with Zephaniah the second priest,
Followed by the three doorkeepers.

Then he made Gedaliah the son of Ahikam,
The son of Shaphan, governor over the people.
While he remained in the land of Judah.

After the army captains heard that the king of Babylon made Gedaliah governor,
They came to Gedaliah at Mizpah.

So, it was that the army captains: Ishmael the son of Nethaniah,
Johanan the son of Careah, Seraiah the son of Tanhumeth the Netophathite,
And Jaazaniah the son of a Maachathite,
Took an oath before them and their men to fight.

Then Gedaliah said to all these men,
"Do not be afraid of the servants of the Chaldeans.
Dwell in the land and serve the king of Babylon too,
And it shall be well with you."

Thus, it happened in the seventh month,
That Ishmael the son of Nethaniah,
The son of Elishama, of the royal family, came with ten men and struck.
Alas, the person they struck was Gedaliah.
Followed by some Jews and Chaldeans at Mizpah, from that time.

Indeed, all the people, small and great,
And the captains of the armies,
Arose and went to Egypt to attack and regroup,
For they all were afraid of the Chaldeans.

Now it came to pass in the thirty-seventh year of Jehoiachin's captivity,
That the Evil-Merodach king of Babylon showed him some more mercy.
Indeed, Jehoiachin- former Judah king in prison garments,
Was given daily food provisions to keep him not famished.
Alas, Jehoiachin never escaped the prison and forced captivity,
Thereby ate food every day until he died in that Babylon city.

www.ingramcontent.com/pod-product-compliance
Lightning Source LLC
Chambersburg PA
CBHW041819090426
42811CB00009B/1042
* 9 7 8 0 6 4 5 7 3 4 2 8 7 *